Dales People at Work

Hilary Gray

GREAT NORTHERN

Published by Great Northern Books,
Holebottom Farm, Hebden, Skipton, North Yorkshire, BD23 5DL.

Copyright © Hilary Gray and Great Northern Books 1999

ISBN: 0 906899 89 3

Cover design: Blueprint Marketing Services, Ilkley
Design and layout: Trevor Ridley
Printed by B.R.Hubbard Ltd (Dronfield)

British Cataloguing in Publication Data
A catalogue record for this book is available from the British Library

CONTENTS

INTRODUCTION

The biggest problem in compiling a book on Dales people is not in deciding who to include but who to leave out. In almost any Dales community there is such a diverse range of self-motivated businesses, diversification and pastimes that it would be impossible to do justice to them all.

Here, Hilary Gray has talked to a selection of Dales people who might no doubt have found a way of making a more lucrative living had they moved to a city environment. It has been their choice to live and work in the area they know and love and, significantly, that is a decision that not one of the people she interviewed has regretted.

THE DOCTOR:
Often in cities doctors need people with them to protect them on night work. One of the joys of working in the Dales is that doctors get to know their patients so much better
(Dr Barry Brewster, retired GP)

THE BREWER:
It probably would have been easier to operate from a city but I have a very strong desire to stay living and working in around Masham. I had to do a lot of heart-searching when we moved house - two and a half miles up the road
(Paul Theakston, Black Sheep Brewery)

DRAMA STUDENT:
It's lovely living in the Dales but you don't appreciate it when you're younger - you take it all for granted and think it's boring because there's nothing to do. But you're really lucky being brought up somewhere like this rather than somewhere in the city
(Katie Barker, Harrogate College)

STONE WALLER:
When I first started walling I worked for two bob an hour – 10p now – and gradually worked up to when I retired I got seven quid, which is nothing compared to some tradesmen but I was satisfied
(Geoff Lund)

CASTLE CUSTODIAN:
You get the odd person who says it's only a pile of stones but you can't really get through to people like that. Those who are interested in history appreciate their surroundings
(June Haines, Richmond Castle)

THE ARTIST:
I'm particularly interested in this area because it's familiar – it's what I know and am emotionally attached to. Even if I were to live away again I wouldn't like to think I'd never come back. I always want to maintain a link with people and places here, it's where my roots are
(Katharine Holmes)

PHOTOGRAPHERS:
Living in a remote location means we're constantly exploring new ways of making a living. Our work means we can have a certain amount of freedom. If it's a nice day we can go for a walk as long as we make up for it at a later stage
(John and Eliza Forder)

CAVE RESCUER:
Any member of any rescue team would say that what they lose in money they gain in life experience. You can be called out and because of the team's input that person is alive today
(David Gallivan)

COUNTRY VET:
Nearly all my time is spent out of surgery. I would hate to give up the cattle work. I couldn't work in an urban practice
(Richard Sutcliffe, Bishopton Veterinary Group)

COMPUTER EXPERTS:
Even in winter we can go outside the office, hear the robins sing and watch the squirrels. We've had pairs of deer walking through the car park. You're just not going to get that in a city
(Simon Fern, Daelnet)

SCHOOL CHAPLAIN:
During term time I used to call my job as chaplain 'salvation by perspiration', you never really stopped. But from a point of view of discipline there was no comparison with teaching in an inner city school in a rough area
(Norman Daniels, former chaplain of Giggleswick School)

THE DOCTOR Dr Brewster of Settle

Until his retirement five years ago, Dr Barry Brewster (68) has been a practising GP for over thirty years in and around Settle. In 1991 a television series featuring his work was filmed by the BBC and an accompanying book The Doctor - Just another year *was published. Dr Brewster's wife, Scottie, the practice nurse for many years, retired at the same time as her husband. Their elder daughter is a nurse who worked for the International Red Cross in Armenia and the Sudan until she married three years ago and gave birth to their first grandchild. Son John and younger daughter Katie are both osteopaths.*

After I qualified at Trinity College, Dublin, I seemed destined to become an obstetrician. I was working in the Rotunda Hospital, a huge midwifery hospital, when a doctor friend of mine rang up my home in Leeds – it just so happened that particular weekend I was at home – to tell me there was a general practice in Settle which needed another partner and would I be interested.

The practice was run by two brothers, David and Tony Hyslop. Tony fairly suddenly upped and went to Nova Scotia leaving his brother therefore desperately looking for a prospective partner.

In those days hospital doctors had little knowledge of general practice. The hospital was your little empire and general practice was something that existed outside. I came up here and saw this practice and found it interesting but I was in the middle of some post graduate degrees and that meant another nine or ten months' work in Dublin. That was in effect saying no to this job because in those days it was difficult to get locums even for a fortnight's holiday, never mind nine months.

As chance would have it when I got back to Dublin I was having a pint of Guinness in the Lincoln's Inn pub and one of my friends Ted happened to be listening to my tales of the weekend about the practice. He told me that his father had retired from the army about a year before, was getting very

itchy feet and might be prepared to do the locum job. He did so and held the practice with David Hyslop for just under a year while I completed my post graduate studies. If Ted hadn't walked in to the Lincoln when I was telling the story, I wouldn't be in Settle today.

When I first came here in March 1962, the surgery was the front two rooms of the house we still live in. I had to buy the house because it contained the surgery. If you remember Dr Findlay and Doctor Cameron I was virtually Doctor Findlay. For quite a number of years, the front hall was the waiting room, separated by one door from the present dining room, then in use as the consulting room.

My partner David Hyslop had a similar set-up at his home 150 metres away. Because we covered such a large area he would go to one end of the practice and I would go to the other. Having said that, we would often cross and arrive in the same village but as things developed we got a bit more organised.

When I first arrived I had no yardstick of general practice at all. There was no appointment system and as one patient left the next would come in. I'd have no idea who I would be dealing with until a head appeared round the door. Patients used to crowd into the hall, the first arriving half an hour before surgery started so they could be first in the queue and some arriving after surgery finished so they could just come in at the end.

Patients even used to walk into the kitchen just before lunch when I was still out on my rounds and say to Scottie, 'Is 'e back?' She was once disturbed by a knock on the bathroom door.

After an extraordinarily long time, about three or four years, I thought there must be a better way. I then divided the dining room with a wooden partition into a five-seater waiting room and a reception room, employed a receptionist and introduced an appointments system. Appointments were better for everybody's

Dr Brewster pays a routine visit to Castleberg, a local nursing home. The Settle practice covers over 300 square miles
PHOTO: DAVID SECOMBE

convenience and you could have patients' files out ready before the surgery started. It was all quite simple commonsense, as most good solutions are. Before that, Scottie used to be on phone duty 24 hours a day so it was a very tying job but we were very happy doing it. It was a way of life.

After about six years here, as we acquired more dogs and more children, things were getting a bit crowded. I heard that the Folly, an imposing building in Settle, was being vacated by its tenant. I managed to rent the ground floor and again I put up some wooden partitions and made a decent sized office. The large room which contained a lovely old fireplace became the waiting room.

David Hyslop was then approaching retirement but he agreed to move his surgery from his home very willingly which I thought was very noble of him. The new arrangement was much more satisfactory in some ways but the soundproofing wasn't terribly good. Anyone speaking in a consulting room in anything louder than a whisper could be clearly heard in the adjacent waiting room. We tried to solve the problem by play-

ing classical music. Scottie overheard the reaction from one waiting patient : 'Sittin' in 'ere's like bein' in a bloody mausoleum.'

But at least at the end of the day, I closed the door and walked home which was really quite something. It was a much more organised feeling. We were also by that stage in partnership with Dr Clegg of Long Preston but six years after moving to the Folly, David retired and to my surprise Dr Clegg retired as well, both within six months of each other. This left me on my own for a few months which was fairly hectic and I realised I would have to find some new partners quickly.

By that time general practice training had started so I had several trainees through my hands. Two of the best were Dr

Eric Ward and Dr John Lewis. They finished their hospital jobs within six months of each other and became my new partners.

I read about a scheme whereby we could cost-rent a new medical centre, a purpose built building. Medical centres are planned, built and paid for by the GPs who work in them as opposed to health centres which had had their problems. For doctors to build their own places was something very new. Within fifteen months we had planned, built and moved into the new premises at Townhead in November 1976. That was a terrific move. In 1982 the practice won a competition for the best functional surgery building in the United Kingdom.

General practice here in the Dales is a different ball game in many ways compared to that of an inner city. A city practice will probably have at least 90 percent of its patients within a mile or two of the surgery. Although traffic problems may be fairly great, that's their total area. Our area is enormous by comparison – over 300 square miles – so we do quite a lot of travelling, although much less now than we used to because general practice is now much more orientated towards the surgery.

We used to have enormous rounds. You'd have a phone-in first thing in the morning for about half an hour and then you'd make up your list and drive off. Typically on a Tuesday morning I went to Langcliffe, Stainforth, Horton and then back through Helwith Bridge to Austwick and sometimes Clapham. Then I'd race back home, grab a bowl of soup for lunch before doing surgery from 1.30 until about four o'clock. After that I'd do a few visits, have a quick a cup of tea and then start surgery again at 5.30 which used to go on until all sorts of hours. Then you would have your paperwork at the end of that. But I enjoyed every minute of it.

When there were just two of us we'd be on duty pretty well all the time. My half day was Wednesday which meant I was off from noon until about 11pm the same evening. At weekends, we would alternate so that from Saturday lunchtime until Sunday night you were off or on.

Years ago we used to have hard winters. I remember visiting a farm up above Horton. I'd managed to get the car through the snow up the road through Newhouses and I stopped at the farm gate. There were tremendous snowdrifts and it was blowing a blizzard. There was no way I was going to get the car up to the farm. I was about to set off and walk through very deep snow when an old horse appeared out of the mist and stood by the gate. I climbed on to the gate and got on the back of the horse with my little black bag and it turned around and trun-

dled quietly up the steep curvy lane and delivered me to the farm. I saw the old lady, had a cup of tea and a nice talk with her, then I got back on that grand old horse which brought me back down to the car again.

In the sixties when it was snowing I did some visits on my daughter's pony, Susie. She was a lovely pony and only died only a couple of months ago at the age of 27. I had one marvellous morning during which I did three visits instead of doing about fourteen racing round in a car. Perhaps the old days had their advantages!

Recently, night work has been a bit of a bone of contention. In this area of the country I always quite enjoyed it, if that's the right word. That didn't mean to say I didn't cuss when the phone went off at 3 o'clock in the morning but there was always a reason. I've never been called out on a wild goose chase at night. Although it may not have been medically significant when I got there one understood why the patient thought it was medically critical.

The city boys have quite a problem with unnecessary night calls with the most ridiculous demands by the public. Some of course are genuine calls but there is also a problem with security. Often in cities doctors have to have people with them to protect them on night work and a lot of lady doctors are unwilling to go out on night calls.

The style of medicine in a city is different from the country. If a patient comes out of the surgery in a city or even in a suburban area, once they're in the street they're anonymous. Whereas if you go to the surgery here a lot of people will see you and know you because of this small population.There's nothing wrong with that, indeed it's a very healthy way of life because people sympathise. One of the advantages or joys in a way is that doctors get to know their patients so much better. You know mum and dad and the kids and their family history.

Urban practitioners will do very little casualty work because patients can quite reasonably go down to the casualty hospital whereas here we do a lot of casualty work, stitching or treating the odd carbuncle or abcess or whatever. If a farmer comes in with a gash, hopefully he waits only a few minutes with us before he's stitched. He wants to be quick, he wants to get back on his tractor in half an hour and by our means he can be. But if he goes to casualty he's in for a long ride and if the injury isn't severe, he may have to get himself down there. In our sort of set-up, one has to think about immediacy of care quite a lot.

The TV programme was filmed in 1990 and six half hour

episodes were shown in 1991. The same team run by Jeremy Mills had done a series on a vet in western Scotland the previous year, then the BBC got the idea of doing a series on a rural general practice. They looked at practices all over the country and then whittled them down to about ten.

After we'd had a couple of visits from them and Jeremy Mills, the producer, had come stayed the night here, we suddenly realised they were getting serious. When he said they wanted to feature this practice we had to think hard how we were going to go about that. It's a very difficult ethical problem – how do you suddenly turn up on a patient's doorstep with a camera team? However, they were a marvellous crew and they established a wonderful rapport with the patients and it seemed to come across well.

They came up from London at various times during the course of the year. We didn't tell them when there was anything in particular going on, they just arrived and I think that was what made the programme score because it was just exactly as the day happened. Nothing was laid on or made up. I didn't deviate from my round at all to accommodate anything which might have looked better. Out of the programme one of my patients old Willie became a bit of a star, but that's just the way it happened.

When Jeremy asked me to do the book, I presumed I had a couple of years to think about it but was told it had to be launched at the same time as the programme was screened. They were already about half way through filming so in fact it gave me about three and a half months. That was a fairly traumatic period but there was only one way to do it and that was to go up into the attic and write longhand. There's quite a business to writing a book – it's not just writing it but having it edited then correcting proofs and working to a deadline. It opened my eyes! Even getting all the paper into the warehouse on which to print the book – I had never thought of all that. It did rather concertina matters. In fact it was just one big rush!

The practice has changed. Patients' expectations, doctors' expectations and the pace of life has changed. The paperwork and bureaucracy are pretty awful now and I think employ far too many people at area and hospital level. They keep trying to do something about that but I don't think they ever will. They change areas of bureaucracy but people just move sideways into other jobs with another title. Obviously an administration is necessary but it requires careful commonsense construction, so that it really facilitates good medical practice as opposed to frustrating it.

One of Dr Brewster's patients, Willie, became something of a celebrity as a result of the TV series but the programme was filmed exactly as the days happened - nothing was specially staged.
PHOTO: DAVID SECOMBE

THE BREWER Paul Theakston of Masham

Paul Theakston (53) is fifth generation of Masham's famous brewing family and opened Black Sheep Brewery in 1992. His wife Sue is the driving force behind the marketing side of the business and eldest son Robert (24) also works for the brewery. Paul and Sue have three other sons Jonathan (22) who is studying at Sheffield, Matthew (20) studying at Manchester and Alex (15), a computer whizz who is still at school in Ripon.

Masham regards itself as the Gateway to Wensleydale. My family have been here certainly since the 16th century, probably as far back as the 14th. I'm very solidly rooted in Masham and always have been.

I left the former family firm T & R Theakston in 1989 after a takeover by Scottish and Newcastle Breweries. There was a job for me with Scottish & Newcastle but it would have meant me upping sticks and moving round and doing the corporate thing, two years here and three years there... I was too old a dog at that stage to learn that trick. Also having been born and bred in a small company I didn't think I would survive comfortably with quality of life in a big company. Hence the decision to leave after the take-over but also the desire to try and re-establish independent brewing in Masham. I was fifth generation of a family that had been involved with the brewery so there was a very strong rooted link into brewing as well as being in Masham.

Those two things conspired to bring us to where we are today. It don't think it would have worked for me if we'd been three miles down the road.

Black Sheep has been trading since the beginning of October 1992. It was at the beginning of 1991 was when we first started on the trail to make it happen, finding premises, buying them and finding equipment. We put the brewery together over the summer of 1992 and brewed our first beer in September of that year. Trial brews were sampled (even the vicar turned up to give it his personal blessing!) and then the first beer was released to the trade. A local Masham pub pipped some sixty initial orders to the post by serving it first.

This premises used to be a maltings. The whole area here, including Theakston's offices next door, used to be Lightfoots, the opposition brewery at Masham. My grandfather came back from the Great War in 1917 minus a leg, and then after the war was over the family bought Lightfoots and turned the brewery element of it into offices and bottling stores, and adding their eight pubs to the Theakston estate. Because he had his own maltings attached to the old Theakston brewery at the other side of town, he sold off Lightfoot's maltings. This building then became the North of England Malt Roasting Company until its closure about twelve years ago, when the buildings were acquired by I'Anson's, one of the local animal feed manufacturers.

Having left Theakstons in May of 1988, I started a dialogue with I'Ansons as I gathered they were prepared to sell the building. Apart from the fact that the buildings were in Masham which was an attraction, the malt kiln, a tall steep-roofed building, was ideal for a brew house. Traditionally, brew houses are built on the tower principle where you start at the top and work down and decant from stage to stage, a system going back into the past when pumps weren't very effective; so breweries relied on gravity just to decant from vessel to vessel. Thus there were as few pumps as possible.

The buildings had been empty for several years and it wouldn't be exaggerating to say that initially the rats outnumbered the humans a hundred to one! Two brewery cats, lots of cleaning and a year later, work began on actually building the brewhouse.

When we were setting up, we wanted to be as traditional as possible. A lot of the plant we installed was second hand and quite old. The three principal brew house vessels, the mash tun, the copper and the hop back, were a matched set we were lucky – lucky from our point of view and sadly from theirs – to acquire from Hartleys Brewery at Ulverston which had closed down.

These vessels are fifty or sixty years old and we reinstalled them in this tower configuration. We also acquired six very traditional fermenting vessels, probably a hundred years old, made of slate, from Hardy Hanson, who operate at Kimberley near Nottingham. They were sitting there long since unused, and they were kind enough to give us them provided we moved them. They're made up of 8ft long by 3ft deep by two and a half inch thick lumps of slate which weigh about 8cwt each – and don't bend, as we discovered!

Three more came from the remnants of Darley's Brewery at Thorne near Doncaster. We bought them for pound notes from the demolition men who were knocking the fermenting room down to make a supermarket. It's ironic, they probably sell our beer on the site now.

Since then we've abandoned hope of finding any more of those, as they're fairly rare birds. As we've grown and expanded we've put in purpose built vessels, stainless steel versions of the same so we have a mix of ancient and modern. We actually hand out a list of where the brewery plant came from and it reads a bit like a Who's Who of English breweries past.

Our original thought was that we would call the new company Lightfoots Brewery as a sort of Phoenix arising from the ashes. Then in January of '92, when it became known that I was acquiring the premises here, our neighbours at Theakstons, who by that time belonged to Scottish Courage or Scottish & Newcastle as it then was, had a think tank and applied to register a number of trade names which I suspect they thought we might use, just as a defensive position from their perspective. They applied to register Lightfoots before we did so we lost out on that and had to find something else.

We looked around for something which had an historical association with Masham and came up with the sheep theme. Masham used to be the centre of the sheep trade. You can still smell sheep on the breeze from the auction mart across the way! There's also a breed of sheep called the Masham so it seemed quite appropriate. The 'Masham Sheep Brewery' didn't sound terribly catchy, so my wife in a flash of inspiration suggested we call it 'Black Sheep Brewery'. It also had the benefit of being lightly tongue-in-cheek about having set up next door to the old family brewery. I have to say they did us a favour; it's worked for us far better than ever Lightfoots would have done.

We've done all sorts of spin-off merchandising and we're world suppliers of puns on sheep themes – you can't tell me any new ones!

From day one we anticipated taking visitors round. Breweries and visitors go hand in hand. Again, we had a bit of a luxury situation because a lot of breweries that are long established find it very difficult indeed from a health and safety point of view and access to get people round while they're actually brewing. They're often quite restricted old buildings, and you don't want people putting their hands on boiling hot vessels. We were able to build visitor facilities in from the start, and although we didn't open it straightaway we put a viewing gallery in the brewhouse with the object of people being able to go up on to the gallery whilst we were working and view from there safely – it's the sight and the smell and the sound. We were able to plan a route which took them through to the fermenting rooms as well without impinging on working areas.

Initially, we started taking people round in the evenings with a small hospitality bar and shop below the offices. After three years we felt confident enough to invest a significant amount in the centre we have now which was opened in May '96. Again, we had the luxury of space. We devoted half the top floor of the maltings building to visitors, by putting a glazed screen up together with all the usual 'offices' – loos, kitchen, bar, fire exits – and a balcony so we had some extra seating. We had about 2,000 sq ft available, so we were able to expand the shop operation and complete the access through to the fermenting room. It's been very busy almost from the day we opened.

During the day time, seven days a week, we have at least one guide on duty, depending on the season, shepherding an hour long tour of up to thirty people. For a modest entry fee they are given an introduction and video then a good tour round the brewery and a half of beer as part of the deal. In the evening, when pre-booked parties come round, there is a more extensive tour if they're interested, two pints of whatever beer they want and a plate of hot food. The bistro is licensed so it's open from ten in the morning to pub closing time at night.

Annually, 50,000 visitors go on the tour but we don't keep a record of shop and bistro customer figures. The fact that we are in Masham, in a tourist area, means that we do get some spin off from there. My wife Sue is heavily involved with the marketing side and the whole visitor centre operation is her conception, design, gestation and birth! Yes, we do sometimes discuss business – usually about 1.30 in the morning in bed!

The greatest compliment that somebody paid us was when

they went round on a tour, told us they had enjoyed it, then added, 'We've seen the museum, now where do you actually brew?' I thought we'd really achieved something then. We brew very traditionally quite deliberately, using good quality old-fashioned materials with no short cuts although it's possibly not the most cost effective way of doing it.

When I started in the sixties there were one or two draymen there whose memories went back to the twenties and they had all sorts of tales about acetylene lamps on the lorries and taking two days to get to the north east. I don't think horses have been used here since the twenties. Five hours with horses wouldn't get you as far as Ripon.

Today, we have about 65 employees. The visitor centre jacked up the numbers employed because it's a retail business and is thus quite labour intensive. We're fairly evenly spilt with about thirty staff in the brewery and the same in the centre although there are also a number of part timers with us in the centre as well.

Black Sheep 'boss' Paul Theakston, fifth generation of Masham's famous brewing family. Paul claims the family and staff are world suppliers of sheep puns!

Two thirds of our output is traditional draught beer and the other third is bottled beer. Probably three quarters of the traditional draught beer is sold to free houses within a 75 mile radius of Masham. We go up into Northumberland to the north and southwards down the coast taking in Tyneside and Teeside and most of the east coast down to Hull and then Barnsley, Huddersfield and Halifax and the ridge of the Pennines and back towards Northumberland. So it's a pretty flexible 75 miles.

We also sell the draught beer to one or two wholesalers so you might find our beer as a guest ale down in Devon, Birmingham or Nottingham. The bottled beer by its nature is easier to travel and that is sold to all the major grocers.

We don't really have secret ingredients but we don't actually nail our recipes on the door of the brewery and invite our competitors to come and take a look! We use traditional varieties of malt and hops, a fair amount of water, and yeast, as do all brewers. The differences are in the varieties of barley and hops and the malting methods. It sounds strange to say this, but the water is almost less important. In days gone by, the main breweries sprang up in places where the water was suitable, and there was a ready a source of good quality water, at Burton-on-Trent for instance. That was very hard water and was suitable for pale ales whereas London was famous for stouts and porter which required a softer water. But there were cottage breweries everywhere.

These days water can be treated. People tend to 'Burtonise' it which is the awful expression which means taking it back to the nominal Burton standard and we are no exception. We have a 300ft deep bore hole for our own water supply so we're independent of Yorkshire Water. It costs about £80 a year for the licence to extract our water.

It probably would be easier to operate from a city but I have a very strong desire to stay living and working in and around Masham. Sue laughed at me fifteen years ago when we outgrew the house in Masham and bought a bigger house in Grewelthorpe two and a half miles up the road. I had to do a lot of heart-searching! I got thrown off the Four and Twenty which is group of 24 good men and true, a centuries old tradition in Masham, although these days it doesn't do a great deal except appoint a church warden and sort out charity money. There are only two things that remove you from the Four and Twenty – one is death and the other is moving out of the parish. So I had to go!

Am I a beer drinker? Yes, I'm a draught bitter man. I don't have to sample it but I do! Fairly regularly...

NATIONAL PARK MANAGER Alan Hulme

Alan Hulme (34) originally from Stockport, is area manager for the south west area of the Yorkshire Dales National Park. His partner Sheila Blackshaw teaches at the local primary school at Malham.

The park is split into two areas, each with a regional manager. Here in the south, I'm responsible for nine other workers. The National Park is a designated area because of its outstanding natural beauty and for its conservation interests as well as its recreational purposes. We are here to safeguard the landscape for future generations.

The role of the area manager and the area management service is that we're the front line staff for the local communities, local individual landowners and farmers, and the first point of contact for local people, working with them to conserve the park and provide for recreation.

All our staff have a formal qualification either in environmental studies, countryside conservation or countryside recreation. I spent three years in Guildford doing a countryside recreation and conservation course involving all aspects of land management. As part of the course I had to do a work placement and was sent here. I was 19 at the time and worked in the Three Peaks area for six months, living in a caravan. I made a lot of friends in the Dales and kept in touch, then applied for a post here after college. I anticipated staying here two or three years before I moved on but I've become settled here.

The lovely thing about the job is that no two days are ever the same because of the range of work involved. A typical day will involve working directly with the area team or with landowners. The area team's workshop is based at Stainforth and four of us area managers share an office at Grassington. On Monday I liaise with the five area team members, each one responsible for different areas of work. That could mean sitting in a meeting with them in the morning or going out to see how the projects are progressing. On Tuesdays and Thursdays I tend to be office based at Grassington catching up on phone calls and paperwork. Wednesday tends to be my day travelling round the Dale seeing farmers and landowners.

This week, for instance, I'm seeing a number of projects that have been put forward for National Park funding by local communities, schemes involving treeplanting, woodland management and footpaths. I'll meet the project applicants and see how the National Park can help. I also need to see two landowners, one of whom wants a historical bridge to be rebuilt and I'm taking a look at some limekilns and old mills. This Friday I'm meeting the Environment Agency which is looking at tree planting and improving habitat for fish along the River Aire.

I spend a lot of time with farmers and landowners on a day-to-day basis either by telephone or site visits, involving a range of projects from problems on rights of way, footpaths and bridleways to walling schemes, woodland management and other ongoing conservation schemes.

I take certain visiting groups out if they're coming to learn about a specific issue such as tourism in Malham or erosion control in the Three Peaks but the number of projects we're involved with limits my time so I may delegate to an officer within my section or a voluntary warden.

Within the area management service we have about a hundred volunteer wardens, 25 allocated to each area. They do a whole range of work for the National Park – lead guided walks, run courses on compass and map work and give talks to schools and other groups. The area team will initiate tree planting schemes or woodland management and the voluntary wardens then undertake a lot of the survey work, monitoring progress.

We also work with volunteer groups such as BTCV (British Trust for Conservation Volunteers), local conservation groups and wildlife trusts. One of the major roles of the area manager is liaising with all the major bodies, both statutory and non-statutory, within an area. For example in the south west area, we work quite closely with the National Trust, English Nature, the Environment Agency and the Forestry Authority where appropriate.

Some people believe the National Park is owned by the nation but that is not true – it's not owned by the nation, neither is it a park in the conventional sense of the word. When the park was designated in 1954, Britain was following on from the American process of designating areas of outstanding scenery as National Parks. That was the right thing to do because National Parks are national assets. Unfortunately, you talk to most locals and one of the biggest gripes they have is the term 'National Park'. It's a working community and living environment and has to support people's livelihoods.

It is very important to remember that the National Park is nearly all privately owned by individuals. The National Park itself probably owns less than one percent of the park. We only own the information centres, the car parks and odd bits of land we have acquired or had left to us. Some of the other National Parks do own larger tracts of land and some have huge landowners like the National Trust who have a very similar remit to the National Park so we know if land is in the hands of the National Trust or English Nature, it's going to be managed along the right lines.

Our policy is not to acquire land but to try to promote good practice in the area. The point we put across to all school groups is that you can visit these areas but at the end of the day it's like your own street – each piece is owned by an individual.

We have had instances where people have come into the centre asking where they can find the slot machines, the fun parks, the swings and the slides. That is some people's perception of a park – somewhere like Alton Towers. That's why we promote understanding of the park through education.

To illustrate that, one of our voluntary wardens was following a family down into Malham Cove. They'd obviously had a fraught journey here and there seemed to be a bit of friction between the mother and the father who were dragging the two

Alan Hulme, area manager for the south west area of the Yorkshire Dales National Park

kids behind. They got to about two hundred yards from Malham Cove and the father turned to the mother and said, 'All this flaming way to come and see a disused quarry'. You hear stories like that and wonder what we're doing wrong!

Each of the National Parks has its own individual character and this is very much a farming landscape, created by farmers in the past. Its drystone walls and its barns are features everybody associates with the Dales. I've visited all the other National Parks now and although they have similarities this is my particular favourite.

National Parks are part of the school syllabus and because of the nearby limestone features, the Malham National Park Centre attracts 40,000 children annually, of all ages. Our last survey said the park attracted 8.3 million visitors but that is visits rather than people so a number of these will be repeat visits. As a farming community the roads really aren't designed to cope with the number of visitors we're getting and parking is a major issue. We like to talk about sustainable development – about people not spoiling what they've actually come to see. But when do villages reach their saturation point?

Because of the sheer numbers of visitors to Malham I have to make sure the footpaths are kept in a suitable condition. We've had to surface the footpaths to the main attractions such as Gordale, Malham Cove and Janet's Foss. Ten years ago it used to be 20 yards wide – just mud. Now hopefully we've benefited the farmers by reducing numbers of people from straying right across the land. We've also hopefully improved visitors' experience of visiting the National Park. The paths are now accessible to a whole range of people from disabled people in wheelchairs through to fully fit decathletes.

The information centre opens less over the winter but the outdoor work goes on all the year round. We try to do all our major projects in the summer months but winter is an ideal time for woodland management. In the autumn months, we're putting our heads together for next year's work so we're all busy beavering away with calculators. Over winter we will work on these projects in more detail and see from where we can attract the necessary funding.

Another role of the area manager is acting as mediator. In certain respects locals see that we are dealing very much with visitors and visitors might see that we're dealing very much with the locals. It's up to us to find a compromise situation.

This farming generation's attitude to visitors and farming practices is changing. Agriculturally, they are a lot more aware of the environmental schemes they can put into practice on their own farms to complement stock rearing. Farming is experiencing particular problems at the moment especially due to BSE and low lamb prices.

This is why we're seeing more farmers providing bed and breakfast and opening their farms to visitors. But I think a lot of them would diversify anyway, they're not in it just for the money, they have sculpted this landscape. It has been cleared by farmers for farming practices and the walls have been built by farmers and there's a great love of the Dales amongst farmers themselves.

A great deal of emphasis since the Second World War has been placed on production sometimes to the detriment of the landscape. Over the last few years that has started to change with resources becoming available for woodlands, walls and barns and conservation schemes. That's where we can help farmers whether through our own schemes or through those other bodies.

We travel round the farms on a regular basis and we try to see the majority of farmers in our area over the year – that can be at the local shows or making ourselves available in the dale or even in the local pub. It's not a bad thing if someone has a grievance because it gives you the opportunity to put forward the case for the National Park. I'm not a planning officer but people know I represent the park and it's a role of the area manager and staff to help promote some understanding. I usually get the stick not from the person who has had a planning application turned down but from a person who's heard about it but hasn't got all the facts!

In thirteen years I haven't had an argument on a farm or in the pub. There's sometimes a bit of huffing and puffing when you first arrive: 'What do you lot want?' but you get through the first couple of minutes and they're sound – that's one of the benefits of the job, they're a pleasure to work with.

The hours of the job do vary considerably. Part of my role is to attend parish meetings at least once a year and I have twenty parishes within my area. We write articles for the parish magazines as well as contributing to the *Dales Magazine* which comes out twice yearly. Our photographs and home telephone numbers appear and people phone me at ten o'clock at night, eight in the morning on Saturdays and Sundays – that's part of my role. The whole idea is that you're the first line of contact and you bring in specialist advice as and when you need it.

I would hate to think how many stiles and footbridges I've built! I had a very good teacher, Al Boughen, who used to work with us and gave me a very good grounding on practical work when I first came here as what they called a field assistant. Nearly all of my time then was spent litter picking, building stiles, gates, footbridges and working with volunteer groups – very much hands-on. I then left and worked for the Public Rights of Way Department for North Yorkshire County Council as their Rights of Way Officer. I returned to the park in '92 as a field supervisor which involved less stile making and more organising for it to be done.

The unfortunate thing is the higher up the ladder you get, the more office based you become and you miss the hands-on part of the job. We all chose the job to be able to work outside. I love dry stone walling – I see it as a three dimensional puzzle and it's so nice to spend eight hours doing some walling but I'm in a position now in which I just can't do that. But the sense of achievement is still the same. Instead of physically building that wall, you are still responsible for having had the work done. Whether I go to an external body to find source of funding and then my own staff or a farmer does the work, I can still look at that wall and say I had a hand in that being rebuilt.

You've got to be in touch with what's happening all the time. We don't want to be seen as Big Brother. We try to involve ourselves with the community as much as possible. We have an education officer who was an ex-teacher and we ask schools, 'What do you want from the National Park as a school?' For instance, each year there's a National Bird Box week around Valentine's day. We go to the local schools and make bird boxes with the children who put them up in their areas.

My partner Sheila teaches at the local school and a lot of the farmers' children go there. And no, the children's marks are definitely not affected if a farmer is giving me a hard time! Because of our work, we're both very much involved with the community and very happy to be living and working in an environment such as this.

WILD BOAR KEEPER Tony Hill

Tony Hill grew up in Nigeria, later returning to his parents' roots in Yorkshire and settling in Wensleydale. He is responsible for reintroducing wild boar to the Yorkshire palates.

My parents bought a house to retire to in Yorkshire having themselves had Yorkshire connections – my father was born in Seaton over at Scarborough. They worked in West Africa and their summer holidays, especially in the latter years, were spent looking for a house in England. We had a number of holidays in Yorkshire and eventually found a house in Wensleydale.

When I left university with a degree in zoology I did the usual thing by going to the big city. I went to London where I worked in sales and marketing. The point was, I couldn't stand London and spent all my free time running to Yorkshire. I eventually found myself spending all my money and running into debt running away for long weekends. So that's how I ended up in the Dales.

I had a tea shop and craft shop and grew mushrooms intensively. After seven or eight years I sold

that business with thoughts of travelling overseas but did a U-turn and came back and had to start again. I was looking for something to do – I was spending far too much time in the pub and decided one Sunday that I was better off following up an article someone had written promoting an open day on their farm in Northumberland where they had just started farming wild boar.

I went up there, took one look at the stud boar and thought: I've got to have one of those. He was such a fierce, wild and handsome fella. Through talking to the Northumberland farmer, I started to recognise an enormous gap that wasn't

Tony Hill recognised a gap in the market and wild boar is now one of the fastest growing delicacies in the Dales.

being filled by UK producers of which there were a handful. I also recognised the fact that there was room for me to coordinate the supply and sales of all these animals being produced into a market. People don't want seasonality they want continuity.

I set about selling other people's meat for them and at the same time producing my own animals to follow on from that. So it all got going simply from spotting a gap in the market. When I first started to become involved, the trade was confined to a few of the more adventurous farmers but nowadays, game is gaining in popularity and the demand for meats is on the increase.

Wild boar are effectively like a domestic pig with a lot more adrenaline. It's like comparing beef to venison. You're dealing with an animal that is domesticated to an extent but the biggest hurdle for anybody getting into wild boar is the fact that you require a Dangerous Animals Licence and people have to do their research. Although there is now considerable information and consultancy from the British Wild Boar Assocation you have to go through the bureaucracy of getting a licence which to a lot of people would be extremely off-putting.

The biggest problems really are from the point of view of handling the animals. A boar is a pig who loves food so most of your handling is done with a bucket but at the same time they're very highly strung animals, easily spooked and if you don't watch it they're crawling up walls. Slaughtering is a big problem for us because a lot of slaughterhouses simply won't touch them. They're extremely quick animals with impressive teeth on them and they look aggressive. Most people are rather fond of pigs, finding them intelligent, domestic beings on a par with dogs. Wild boar are different in looks, temperament and taste. They are taller, leaner, fierce by instinct and covered with strong dark body hair.

Somebody once wanted to film them and I was moving them round with a bucket. When a pig gets really wound up, rather like a dog, it starts salivating and one bit me on the bum but it was more a question of 'Give me the food!' They can be dangerous, especially at farrowing and they have few youngsters. Five or six is a common size for a litter. I generally run twenty sows and a couple of boars.

In times gone by wild boar was one of the heraldic 'Beasts of the Chase' and was a delicacy at many a medieval banquet before being hunted to extinction in Britain 300 years ago. Richard 111 made the White Boar his emblem so it's appropriate that it should be reintroduced to this area.

Visit any pub or restaurant in the area which has the slightest interest in 'game' and you will find wild boar on the menu – wild boar sausages, roasts and stir fries. Chefs buy all they can use and cooks at home are seeing it as an original alternative to spice up jaded palates. It is probably the fastest growing delicacy on the market.

For anyone who is bored stiff with watery, tasteless meats and for the health conscious consumer, it's a chance to taste real food. The animals roam free in their natural habitat, feeding and routing. They are not forced to take artificial hormones or growth promoters so their muscle develops slowly, influencing the taste of the meat. It takes four times as long to rear a wild boar than it does a pig. But as I mentioned before, wild boar is to pig what venison is to beef. The meat is rich and succulent, slightly more like beef than pork – but really in a class of its own. Because the animals seem so tough and fearless you might imagine the meat to be stringy too but in fact it is noticeably tender. For the farmer looking to diversify I wouldn't hesitate to recommend wild boar as being low in maintenance and high in profit.

Wensleydale Wild Boar Breeders supply Harrods as well as supermarkets up and down the country and there's such a demand that there is often not enough meat to go round. Potential customers who have difficulty tracking it down can simply pick up the phone and order a selection of wild boar products to be delivered to the door or to Beavers in Masham.

To order from a selection of wild boar meats,
tel : 01677 460239

THEATRE MANAGER Bill Sellars

Bill Sellars has been in the entertainment business for 53 years and is now manager of The Georgian Theatre Royal and Theatre Museum in Richmond. He is responsible for all that goes on, both on the stage and off it, as well as planning the programme.

I STARTED my theatre life in an army concert party in 1945 in India where we toured for two years. After that, I went into repertory theatre in Northampton and Derby. I wanted to be a serious actor but after the concert party I did anything that was going, including stand-up comedy. One of my concert party colleagues, James Perry, went on to write a number of television situation comedies such as *Dad's Army*, *Hi-di-Hi* – because he'd been a Butlin's redcoat – and *It Ain't Half Hot Mum*. I used to watch that programme wondering which one was supposed to be me!

In 1958 I went into the BBC as a director/producer where I stayed for 32 years and in 1990 I came here to Richmond to retire, having been involved with the area for about twelve years working with the BBC. I had moved from the south and the idea was that I would potter around, have a greenhouse and grow a few tomatoes. I was born in Derbyshire so I felt I was coming home to the hills and dales of the north – and I wasn't a total stranger to the weather!

A year after my arrival I was told this theatre was looking for a new director/manager and would I be interested in taking it over. It was a part time post – they said! By this time, I'd had a year of pottering and thought it might be fun to go back to my theatre roots. I'd been involved in the business for 47 years, so it wasn't something new and different. But instead of actually treading the boards, or being involved in the practical side of the theatre, here was an opportunity to do work on the administration side, not only in the theatre itself but in the theatre museum. Our theatre museum deals with 18th century theatre

– this one in particular – and it is the only one outside London.

In my third year of my working here we were awarded one of the first Heritage Lottery grants to refurbish the museum which is now up and running. This little theatre is a main exhibit of the museum but not only is it a museum, it is a working, practical theatre.

Its origins go back to a man called Samuel Butler, a travelling showman/actor/manager who walked from town to town with his own company of players. He built the theatre in 1788, leasing the land from the local council. Every town had its own playhouse and its intent when it was built was public performance.

We now have air cooling but it can still be very hot in the theatre so you can imagine what it must have been like when it was originally opened in 1788 and 400 people would sit through performances which would last for six hours. An actor/manager would only come here once a year in autumn so it was a great occasion. The audience of the day would save up their shillings all year to see the performance. The price of a seat in one of the boxes was three shillings, in the pit two shillings.

There are only 186 seats now. Originally, there were no chairs, only benches and not only were there more benches in the pit than nowadays, they were smaller in order to cram more people in. All of that was part of the atmosphere of 18th century theatre.

The people in the gallery would have what was known as a kicking board which is just offset from the rear of the gallery front to create a gap for resonance. They would kick it to show their appreciation – or otherwise. You can imagine them being in here for six hours and they couldn't easily get out except by clambering over each other. There were no toilets so the men would bring zinc cans with them and use them, then slot those cans into the gap between the front of the box and the kicking board – and the contents would end up on the audience below.

Bill Sellars, manager of the Georgian Theatre Royal and Theatre Museum came to Richmond to retire...

The theatre at one point was closed for immorality. That has never happened in my day – they're much better behaved – nor do they have to bring zinc cans!

The theatre closed in 1848 when the council took it over, ripping out the theatre completely and flooring over the downstairs seating to the stage. It was then used for all sorts of purposes, including a corn merchant's premises when the panels from the theatre boxes were removed to store sacks of corn. The building was also used as an auctioneer's, a storage for waste paper during the war – all kinds of things.

The void under the floor was used at one time to store wine. The large entrance door which we still have today had been constructed to roll the wine barrels through.

Investigation underneath the stage revealed wooden runners to enable the trapdoors to slide. The Georgians loved that kind of trickery and that was when it became clear that the building had been a theatre. Further investigation found the remains of painted canvas behind the benches.

Slowly but surely after more than a hundred years of closure, the theatre was refurbished and reopened in 1963. Layers and layers of paint were scraped off until they revealed the colour which was right for the Georgian era. Under layers of paint, lettering was discovered above the boxes which turned out to be the names of playwrights so these were also restored.

We now stage about eighty public performances a year. It isn't a Monday to Friday theatre, it's a one night stand theatre or two nights at the most for professional touring companies, local companies, operatic societies, dramatic societies, you name it, they all hire the theatre from time to time.

The theatre is run by about 150 staff who are all voluntary with the exception of two paid staff, myself and my assistant.

Without the voluntary staff we could not open. They do everything from putting the pit cover on (in front of the stage) to selling tickets in the box office and guiding groups round the theatre. The staff in the shop selling items of interest are all voluntary as are the museum staff working on the archives upstairs. When you consider the theatre museum is open morning and afternoon and we need two guides in the morning and two in the afternoon, you can soon get through your availability of guides.

Thankfully, the theatre survives. We have two seasons a year, April until July and September to Christmas. Naturally, the theatre struggles with 186 seats. You can sell every seat in the house and still make a loss. Over a year, these losses have to be made up with grants from local council, the Arts Board, town councils, county councils, district councils – fund raising of all kinds, but it gets by on a knife edge all the time.

There is a wide diversity of programme. The mix ranges from Spanish dancing to ballet to classical drama to popular drama and classical music to popular music and one-man shows. It's a community theatre which means you have to cater for all tastes, not your own personal taste. That makes the job and the programming interesting.

Like so many others, we have a lottery bid in the pipeline for a major refurbishment – no structural changes in the actual theatre because it is a Grade One listed building. Renovations will include a new staircase and a lift to take wheelchairs, as well as new toilets and cloakrooms which are presently quite Dickensian. In the lottery bid we have to look at two aspects. One, to maintain the historical importance of the building but also to maintain a working theatre. It is still a theatre, it is not a museum. If it's financed by the lottery, then all the more reason why it will remain a community theatre.

There are two schools of thought – people who would love it to remain a museum and just take people around but that is not its function, it must be kept as a theatre. At the same time, it must have a museum quality about it so that people can come and look. That really makes my job very difficult at times!

It is a unique building, there's no doubt about it and people come here from all over the world. It is the oldest working theatre in its original form in the country. It is not the oldest working theatre – that is the Bristol Old Vic but that has been changed and modernised. This, give or take a few changes like chairs or cushions on the benches, is the oldest.

I am now in my seventh year here – so much for retirement. I've never worked so hard in my life but that's part of the pleasure.

One of Geoff's landscape photographs:
Cattle by Dewpond near Malham

Once you got used to it, your hands weren't so bad. Gritstone's a shocker for wearing your hands out but gritstone's a better shape. Not everyone can wall limestone. A stranger to limestone will leave big holes all over because he hasn't got the eye for it. You almost have to be bred into limestone to wall it.

Walling's a wonderful thing on a beautiful day. I'll admit it's not nice on a rough day but those days have gone now. I don't have to work in the rain anymore.

I used to want beautiful sunny days for my photography but sometimes they can be too contrasty. I've started to study clouds and use a graduation filter and I nearly always use a warm up filter especially for portraits. It makes the difference between cold and warm. I use a monopod nearly all the time. I'm also using blue filters because people want a colourful picture. I'll wait ages for the sun to come out to get the perfect picture.

Although it's important to look into the distance before you take a photograph, I've come to the conclusion that the foreground plays a tremendous part. I'm going to take my own flowers up to Trollersgill. I once took a photograph of an owl, but it was stuffed – I just found a hole in a tree and put the owl there with a mouse in its beak!

I'm always looking for the perfect setting. Round the back of Penyghent is a big rock square which is a perfect frame for a picture. Sometimes I might cheat a bit by taking off a tree branch here or there...

I think I'm very lucky to have been given a gift of seeing things, balancing something and weighing it up. When I was younger I used to be very sensitive. Not any more – you can call me what you like as long as my dinner's ready!

CASTLE CUSTODIAN June Haines

June Haines (61) is head custodian at Richmond Castle and has been involved with the Department of the Environment, later English Heritage, for 31 years. Her husband was custodian at Mount Grace Priory until he retired but is delighted that June is still working! They live at Swainby, a sixty mile round trip from Richmond Castle, and have two married daughters and four grandchildren.

My job involves looking after Richmond Castle. Not the grounds as such, the grass cutting is out to contract but I have to report that it's being done correctly and that the contractor is up to scratch. I'll report on any vandalism or break-ins or any repairs that might be necessary.

English Heritage came into being in 1984. Before that it was the Department of the Environment and before that it was the Ministry of Public Buildings and Works. Some people get a bit confused between English Heritage and the National Trust. We're government funded but the National Trust is totally a charity. They deal more with houses, gardens and land whereas English Heritage is more involved with ruins – monasteries, castles and monuments. English Heritage give out an awful lot of money in grants for churches, barns, listed buildings and so on.

My job is dealing with the public. English Heritage run a membership scheme which I try to persuade visitors to join. Once they're members they very often rejoin a second or third year. It entitles them entry to all properties within England that belong to English Heritage.

When my husband became the custodian of Mount Grace Priory which is an English Heritage site, I did two days' relief for him at the weekends. At the same time, I was a cook at the village school at Ingleby Arncliffe. Then the custodian here at Richmond Castle retired so I applied. I've been here since 1990 but my husband started with the old Ministry of Works so in

effect I've worked for them for 31 years. Normally with English Heritage you would retire at sixty but because I worked for the Department of the Environment I had a reserved right so I could go on to 65 on an annual assessment. Hopefully, I'd have to do something pretty drastic before they'd get rid of me!

I spend my time between the office, helping serve in the kiosk and dealing with visitors. This year we have tried to delegate and concentrate on our own little departments but at the end of the day it's my head on the block if we don't meet our targets and so we all help each other.

When you're dealing with the public there's always problems. Even today, there was a gentleman who insisted that English Heritage and National Trust should join forces. I was trying to explain that they will never ever do that because one is a charity and one is government funded but he just argued my point. I just could not get through to him. On the other hand you get people who are really friendly and who'll take a joke.

Sometimes when people say, 'Can I have two pensioners?' I'm tempted to say 'Sorry, we don't have any pensioners left.' You get to know who you can say things to and who you can't. You can tell if they have a sense of humour or whether they would take offence.

One day, it was pouring down with rain and a man walked in the shop. He was wearing an anorak which was zipped up and he had a camera with all the connections and a zoom lens sticking out at the front. All he said was, 'It's my camera' and so I trotted out the old Mae West joke, 'Oh, I thought you were just pleased to see me.' I knew by his face I could get away with it!

We get about 65,000 visitors a year. That includes school parties which are free. We keep a record of visitors and we're open throughout the year, seven days a week. In the summer we work a rolling roster so that one person isn't always working weekends. The only days the monument is closed is

Christmas Eve, Christmas Day and Boxing Day. We opened on New Year's Day for the first time last year. It went a little bit against the grain with me, I can tell you! But as I drew the short straw last year, I hope I won't have to do it this year!

Richmond is an early Norman castle built in 1071 for Alan the Red, one of William the Conqueror's trusted men who helped him invade England. He was granted this little bit of land and this castle was built for him as a stronghold for the north against the Scots. There have been no battles or sieges here, it was just a royal stronghold.

The keep is intact and you can get right to the top – there are 133 steps. On a good day there are beautiful views up the dales or east towards the coast. You can see for miles. We get a lot of people who spend a lot of time up there just walking round and round looking at the views.

There are extensive Norman ruins up to the East Scollans Hall, one of the first stone built halls in a castle. Up to that point they were wooden – mott and bailey. Americans always want to buy the castle stone by stone and take it home. If it was mine, I might sell it to them!

The majority of people come on a trip to Richmond, see the keep from the market square and so they come and visit the castle. School children often bring their parents back with them after they've been here on a school visit. Most people enjoy it. You do get the odd person who comes and says it's only a pile of stones but you can't really get through to people like that. Those who are interested in history appreciate their surroundings.

We have 65,000 annual visitors, really condensed into six months but we're here to answer all their questions. In the winter when we're quieter I do go round with people sometimes giving them a sort of guided tour but in summer it just gets so busy. In summer from the 1st of April until the end of October we're open from 10 until 6 and in winter it's 10 until 4. In winter we close for an hour's lunch break but in summer we have more staff on so we can cover it. I'm full time throughout the year. Helen in the shop is full time throughout the summer and we have Pat who does four days in the summer and works part time in the winter.

The castle is famous – or infamous, whichever way you look at it, for conscientious objectors who were imprisoned here in the First and Second World Wars. There are eight cells and you can see where there have been six bunks in each cell. They're mentioned in the guide book but it's not open to the public because there's graffiti there. It's in such a delicate state that

June Haines is responsible for major events - as well as ordering loo paper

the cells have been locked up and left so the humidity and the light is preserving them. We think my office which is a later addition to the keep, built in Victorian times, used to be the guard room for the prisoners. You can see where there have been bunks. It has been a later addition to the keep, built in Victorian times.

When I first started with my husband at Mount Grace he was what they called a single custodian. He cut the grass and had a few guide books, pencils and maybe a few rubbers and post-cards and that was it. He kept a diary which he called *From Biscuit Tin to Electronic Till* because he used to have his money in a biscuit tin on a shelf and a bag slung over his shoulder. It's all changed immensely but you just gradually absorb it and you don't think of the change. Now it's all trading and we're on computers – except mine is away at the moment because it wouldn't work! I think I'm too old for electronics!

The castle does a lot of re-enactments and big events. I'm not really involved with the organisation as such until it's all coming together a couple of days beforehand. The big events are organised in London and I get information about everything that will be coming, including the Portaloos! With being close to a garrison (Catterick) we have in the past done a lot of army events such as beating the retreats.

Thankfully, we don't have a lot of trouble with vandals. Occasionally, agile young kids can get up the wall and we've had the odd unauthorised barbecue in the corner! There's an English Heritage flag on the top of the keep and one day I came in and it had gone. Somebody had shinned up the flag post as a dare. The flag is changed when it's a Royal birthday or anniversary the Union Flag goes up about twenty times a

View of Richmond Castle and the bridge, from the river.
ENGLISH HERITAGE PHOTOGRAPHIC LIBRARY

year. I have a list of all the dates so I'm the flag changer. This is classed as a Royal Castle. Henry the Second finished the keep. There were barracks along the west wall and Baden Powell was there for two years so we get a lot of scout and guide services. On St George's Day they always come here and march to the church.

There's a legend of the drummer boy. In the 17th century, the army was here and there's a tunnel supposedly from Richmond Castle to Easby Abbey and the drummer boy went down and drummed and the soldiers walked on the top and he suddenly stopped never to be seen again. According to the legend, he's still there. Halfway between here and Easby which is about a mile along the river, there's a drummer boy stone and that's where the drums supposedly stopped. In the bottom of the keep there are steps which are paved over at the moment because the dungeons are too dangerous to comply with health and safety regulations but that's where he's supposed to have gone down.

We help out at other English Heritage sites such as Middleham Castle and Barnard Castle when there's a special event. I like meeting and working with people. I don't know that I'd like to be on a site where there's only one person. The worst part at Richmond is cleaning the toilets and we have all the keep to sweep but we don't do it all in one fell swoop we do a staircase at a time. We just keep on top of it. We're responsible for everything from ordering the loo paper.

A consignment of lollipops have arrived today for the shop and unfortunately, they're all broken! We have a buying team in London who do all the buying and organising then in January or February each year all the custodians go down and there's a big exhibition and you choose what you want but they like to keep it within the theme. Mine mainly relates to Norman kings and queens.

You absorb the history as you go along. It has given me more of an interest in other properties but I don't visit a lot because in a way it's a busman's holiday although I will do more of that when I retire. At the moment I work full time so I just get two days off and then I've got my washing and ironing!

DALES FARMER John Metcalfe

JOHN METCALFE (60) was born at Holme Farm at Sedbergh where he still farms with his son David (29). John's wife, Ann, is a primary teacher at Lancaster and their daughters are Ruth, a GP and Rachel who is in the police force.

Holme Farm is in the parish of Middleton. We have 120 acres here plus fell grazing rights on Middleton Fell.

We've been open to the public for twelve years. We put our leaflets in tourist offices but we've done less and less advertising as time has gone on. Originally we were hoping to open for free just for the local community. It was surprising how little even some of the local children knew about farming. With the insurance side and the safety aspect we couldn't afford to continue to do it free for everyone but local school, Guide and Brownie groups still come free. We first put a sign up on the road about twelve months ago and that has brought in quite a few people who have been driving past but it's made it a lot more time consuming.

We used to work on the basis of a 2 o'clock tour. Anyone who came earlier than that walked round the nature trail and had a picnic then joined the tour. Now people see the sign and come and expect a tour at any time of day. My son David works on the farm full time now so he gets dragged in to help. My wife Ann is a full time teacher but she helps as well when she's at home or on holiday.

We have about 5,000 visitors a year including schoolchildren. During term time after Whitsuntide we have a school class here

John Metcalfe's farm is open to the public but is still very much a working farm - when he can find the time...

most days. This year two schools came all the way from Liverpool, two from Manchester and one from Newcastle for the day out. They do projects, following what is supposedly the first rural geography curriculum pack produced in Britain. There's also a science based curriculum pack which Ann helped to produce.

Most of the school teachers come armed with a camera and fathers too take pictures of their children holding the animals. In the barn about two thirds of the wall is plastered with letters from the children. They get really excited about the animals.

The nature trail takes the best part of two hours, then they can spend half an hour having a picnic and about an hour and a half going round the farm looking at the animals. The nature trail is a mile and a quarter over the wood tops and back on to the farm again. There's a kingfisher on the river and sand martins nest there as well. Dippers are fairly common and various breeds of wild duck. We have mallard and merganser and herons have been nesting here for the fifth year. We also have a protected badger sett in the wood. There's a hide where you can watch them at feeding time. There are often foxes passing by, tawny owls and a wide variety of field and woodland birds.

On the farmyard we get a lot of children who have never seen, touched or held live animals before. We get loads of special needs children, children from residential centres and young children from playgroups right through to sixth formers.

They ask all sorts of questions. One of the little ones asked, 'How do you tell if it's a boy or a girl?' The Brownie leader answered, 'If it's got a bit extra it's a little boy, if there's a bit missing, it's a little girl.' The children think every cow that has horns is a bull then they'll look underneath it and realise it's a cow!

We have a pony in the field and the children can hand feed the sheep, chickens and pet lambs. Most of the animals are hand reared in the first place which makes them quite used to children.

A little fellow came recently in a wheelchair and the only muscles he could move were his eyelids. We had a chicken which we put on the tray on his wheelchair. We gave it some food and it ate in front of his nose and he actually smiled. That was the first reaction they'd had from him all week. We also get quite a number of blind children who virtually dissect the animal by feeling its shape.

The pigs are the favourites with the children and they love holding the little Pot Bellies. Pigs don't bite – unless children stick their fingers in their mouths! One of the Vietnamese pigs is going to Lancaster as a pet. They can live in the house and are very easy to train. They have a sleeping area, separate feeding area and a separate toilet area and never the three shall mix, given the right conditions and clean straw. But outside they'll wallow in mud and turn your garden over for you – whether you like it or not!

The other pigs are Large White crossed with Landrace. We have a sow at the moment with a litter of four. Pigs are losing money fast. Some farmers are gassing new born piglets because each pig will lose about £30. It's a serious problem.

Feeding all the animals is a morning and night job. We have a caravan park as well and each time the campers come they have their favourite animals and they know their names. Little kids always want to come and help on the farm but that's too dangerous if there's machinery about although we let them come and help with the animal's feeding. Quite a few of the campers will come and join us when the schools are going round.

We have a suckler herd of twelve cows. Each cow produces one calf each year and is allowed to suckle feed her own calf. Any surplus milk is used on the farm as animal feed – for pet lambs over six weeks old, goats, hens and cats. The pigs are happy to help out if there's still any left over!

We have eleven calves at the moment, the youngest six weeks old. We have a Charolais cross, a Simmental cross and a Limousin cross. We used to have about fourteen different breeds but all the dairy breeds have had to go because there's no subsidy on these. We still have Shorthorns, Aberdeen Angus and Belted Galloway.

We 'feed on' calves which are kept as a replacement breeding cow. All the others go to market. The calves are sold at about nine months and the breeding cows remain on the farm until they're about twelve years old.

The cattle are housed in sheds during winter when grass is unavailable and fed both silage and concentrate feed. They also eat a quantity of straw which is used for bedding.

The old ewes off the mountain we cross with Suffolk rams and get Black Faced Suffolk lambs for the meat market. The Rough Fell is the main breeding ewe. If you cross a Swaledale with Blue Faced Leicester you get what's known as a mule gimmer and they have been worth about £100 at six months old but this year it's dropped down to £50. Mules are a highly prolific breeder. If they don't have twins at two years old, they're in disgrace. They often have threes and fours.

The price of lambs this year dropped to only between £3 and

£5 each so we're keeping the remainder hoping the price will rise. Old ewes are fetching £1 or £2 so we're holding on to them as well.

Jet the billy goat is a Golden Guernsey which we do discourage the children from patting because, like all billy goats, he smells! Skippy and Hilda, two of the other goats, are enjoying eating the new silage crop.

We have a peacock and also two youngsters, last year's chicks, a male and a female.

There are thirty hens and about fifteen cockerels. Eric the pet calf has been bottle fed by the children all summer.

We have four dogs in total and we have seven or eight cats which are having kittens all the time. We have day old kittens at the moment but we can't find them! We wanted to keep one on the farm from the last litter but someone took a fancy to it and it disappeared. They're working cats, to control rats and mice. Before we had the cats, there were nine different varieties of birds nesting in the front garden then someone dropped a pregnant cat in and we looked after it...

I was born in the farmhouse here. I'm just over sixty now. The original farmhouse, now a barn, is over 300 years old – there's an old cart in there which I can remember playing on as a lad. The 'new' farmhouse is 150 years old! The road down through the farm is an old Roman road. We get people coming along with metal detectors and they find a lot of tin cans! The road crosses the river by ford and goes through to Tebay and up to Carlisle. Occasionally the walkers have to strip off to get over.

When I was a lad we used to get hard winters. 1947 of course was the worst. But then we didn't have mechanical diggers. About three years ago the lane was full of snow but then they came along with a JCB. We were stuck in here for four days. They say we're in for a hard winter if the trees are laden with berries for the birds but that just means conditions were right in the spring to produce berries later! For years and years we've had loads of berries and had the mildest winters possible so that just doesn't follow.

Four years after I left school in 1958 we got our first tractor, a Dexter. Prior to that, it was all horses. We got electricity the same year and a new tarmac road. We used to use our neighbour's telephone until we got a line of our own about fifteen years ago.

The farming was on a more intensive system for a while but the idea now is to return to more extensification farming with far less stock. We used to do dairy at one point and were fairly heavily stocked with all the pastures divided into paddocks. When the cows moved out, the fertilizer moved in behind them. We moved out of dairy a lot of years ago into the beef side. Beef and sheep go better together rather than dairy cows and sheep because dairy cows and sheep go for the best grass.

The main thing is that we do keep this as a working farm. A lot of these places (open farms) are done up like a dog's dinner but visitors here can see the farm in action, feeding, bedding and so on. Quite often the school parties in particular see stone walling and hedging. We do our own shearing. Each afternoon we put on a demonstration from the middle of June to the end of August and all school parties who come in the mornings get shearing demonstrations. Contractors do our silage but if we put our shearing out to contract we would be out of pocket - fleeces this year are worth only 50 pence each.

There's always plenty to do – repair work and so on. I'm pleased my son has joined me on the farm. He enjoys it, particularly sheep, whereas I was more of a cattle man. The sheep are more viable now because of the BSE business. But now of course, they're in trouble too. It's partly because of the strong pound and export has been difficult. The Russian economy has ruined the price of lamb to a certain extent because lamb skins were worth about £8 each to Russia. Now there's no market there at all.

The export situation is improving slightly because since the end of August they've had a farmers' ferry running about three times a week which carries about 11,000 at a time and when that's fully operational it should ease the lamb prices.

I like farming but otherwise I would have been a science and technology teacher. We do have a holiday – we get four days off at the end of October and go where it's even quieter – to the Isle of Mull. We always managed a week's holiday when the children were small and the neighbours used to look after the farm.

Christmas as far as the animals are concerned is just another day and they still need to be looked after! We are open to the public from the beginning of March to the end of September and the rest of the year is by arrangement – mostly in the car park when people arrive!

THE AUCTIONEER Laurie Kay

*LAURIE KAY has been an auctioneer for 37 years and is assis-
tant manager for Craven Cattle Marts. His wife, Christine, is a
secretary and son Alastair (24) is a vet in Penrith.*

My dad used to be a butcher and we lived in Bolton.
When I was on holiday, I used to come to the market
with him in Hellifield which is where we live now.
He used to come here to buy fat lambs and fat cattle in the sale.
I heard these auctioneers at work and I just fancied the job.

When I left school at sixteen a chap at Hellifield told me, 'If
you want to be an auctioneer you want to go up the hills and
sell on your own, sell to yourself' and so that's what I did. I
used to do a bit of shooting, although I don't bother shooting
nowadays – and I used to practise auctioneering away to myself
while I was walking about.

I came up here to work and used to lodge at Hull House
Farm cottage with Mr Dakin. Before I passed my driving test, I
would come up on a Monday on the train then go back Friday
night. I was an auction clerk then and one day Mr Mawson the
auctioneer told me, 'Come on, you're going to sell these cows
today' and so that was that, that's how I started. I'd be about
seventeen then.

I was a bit nervous the first time because it was sprung on me
but you do your best. Once you get going you're not so bad.
All the buyers help you by giving you a bit of trade for the first
few times while you're starting but after that they'll try and cut
you off by the stocking tops and get them as cheap as possible.
It took a year or two to get the job off properly but I've been
doing it for about 37 years now.

The job involves farm valuations, farm sales, then you have
your auctioneering at the auction marts as well. You meet all
your farmers and have a crack with them, as they say up the
Dales. They're the ones who are paying your wages at the end
of the day. If they don't show any stock, you don't get any
wages.

I do furniture sales as well. We had one this week in
Sedbergh and they always draw buyers from all over the country from as far away as London. We sell livestock at Skipton and
Sedbergh but in addition to that we do farm sales, we sell property, we sell land – we sell anything! We get around a lot.

There's all sorts of different ways people bid – they'll move a
finger, they'll flick an eye, they'll have their hand in their pocket and just move a little finger or else they'll move their head...
you get used to their different movements and you know they
want to bid.

At furniture sales I have had people buying things they
haven't meant to buy because they've moved at the wrong
time. They'd shout, 'No, I didn't bid, sir!' then I'd have to
say, 'Do you mind, Madam, keeping your hands down. I
thought you wanted to be in.' It would turn out she'd been
waving to her friend across on the other seats. If the bidding
has finished and that's happened, you just have to put the item
up for auction again. You give them a bit of a talking to – you
don't get mad with them but it gets them a bit upset and
makes them think I hadn't better do that again! I tell them
next time you do, you're going to finish up with some furniture you don't want! You have to have a crack with the crowd
and I enjoy that side of it.

I sell on Mondays, Wednesdays, Fridays and Saturdays. Odd
Tuesdays I don't sell unless we have a furniture sale. People
don't realise the time you have to spend cataloguing sheep and
cattle and ringing clients up to find out if they're going to
come to the auction. If somebody wants some Texel lambs or
whatever they'll ask if I can find them some because they'll be
there on Wednesday morning so you do your best to ring
round. You know farmers who have them and you ask them if
they'll show some because you think there'll be a bit of trade

that day.

Every farmer now has a LandRover or pickup and trailer whereas years ago hauliers with small wagons would do a lot of hauling for these farmers. Many years ago at Hellifield they would walk the milk cows to the auction and it would take them hours.

When I first started we used to sell a lot of milk cows at Hellifield and also in-calf cows but now things have changed. A lot of in-calf cows used to come down from Scotland to the fort-nightly sale on a Tuesday. There would be five or six hundred here.

They would start arriving on Sunday and we used to have to bed them all up. We employed staff outside to do that. But now you get very few in-calf cows. That's how farming's changed in recent years. In these days, Dales farmers would bring newly calved heifers down in August and September time. There were a lot about then.

The market at Hellifield is shut now but at Skipton we'll get anything from forty to a hundred milk cows. You may get twenty or thirty in-calf cattle and that's it. We sell store pigs and gelt pigs on a Wednesday. Lambs are fetching less and less every day at the moment. There's very little export at the moment and there's no beef export because of the BSE. August until November is our busiest time. You have your gim-mer lamb sales, your store lamb sales, store cattle sales and suckler cow sales.

The paperwork's terrible. You have any amount of forms to fill in now for livestock. Some of the farmers are absolutely fed up of it. They have farm work to do then they come in at night and have to start and do all this paperwork. And it seems to be changing every week. I know we have some new forms coming

Laurie Kay in action at Sedbergh auction mart. Having a 'crack' with the farmers is what it's all about
PHOTO: J & E FORDER

out for these BSE cattle, all new forms. We've had I don't know how many different forms since this job came out.

On an auction day I leave home about quarter past seven. You can be home again at 5, 6 or even 8 o'clock. Some days you can be selling for seven hours a day. Then when you come home you have the telephone ringing. They ring you up and say, 'I have a house full of furniture will you come?' and you have to take an inventory so you know what there is to advertise.

But the job can have its funny moments. I remember one

Thursday afternoon at Hellifield when we were selling fat cattle. They just go round the ring once and then they're out. This beast got round the back of the gate and there was a chap sitting on another gate where they go out. It got him up the backside and he ended up on the beast's head and was taken flying right round the ring, still holding the gate. All these other butchers and farmers were laughing and laughing but this fella wasn't right suited about it! They still laugh about it now.

Years and years ago, we had a chap who used to buy a lot of milk cows and he went a bit funny and couldn't pay. He was from down south and so we went down to collect some debt. I took his car off him and the boss who was with me had brought a wagon and we gathered these cows up and brought as many away as we could. I drove the car home but I got lost and stopped a policeman in the Midlands to ask him the way back to the M6. I didn't realise at the time that the car wasn't licensed and it wasn't even my car.

I once had to go to another spot down south and knock on the door of a farmer who owed the auction mart money. I saw somebody disappearing down the field and it was him – he'd jumped out the back window. But we capped him one day. We left Hellifield about 4am and I took one of the directors down with me. I said to him, 'You go round to the front door and I'll go round the back' and then we had him. We told him we'd come either for some money or stock. We waited and waited and about 9 o'clock he disappeared and ten minutes later, came back with the money. Where he'd got it from, we never did find out.

On the furniture side of things they used to throw out all sorts, roll top desks, sideboards, nice old tables and chairs – they thought they were just rubbish, smashed them up and threw them away on the tip. But you can sell anything nowadays because the car boot industry is booming. Last Tuesday we had nearly six hundred lots and there was only an odd lot or two which weren't sold. You sell it in boxes and these car booters give £1, £2, £3 for it. Then they go off on a Saturday or Sunday with it and sell it on.

Most of the stuff we sell is from estates and house clearances. Some of it fetches more than you would think. On Wednesday there was a drop leaf table at £300 and an oil lamp which made £120. The last sale I had at Hellifield I had a bow fronted corner cupboard which went for £5,500 and I sold a picture at Sedbergh for about £1,200. There was just two fellas wanted it. It was an oil painting and it was torn but it must have been something special.

We have about four or five furniture sales a year. I get a lot of dealers there and I always say if the dealer gives so much you can give a bit more because they have to get profit out of it. We used to have a chap who came here from Burnley who used to send a lot to America and Holland as well. Another chap used to send it to Australia. Pine furniture seems to be a good seller at the moment. They seem to give more if it's painted, mucky and dirty and in a bad state so they can dip the pieces.

At the farm sales you get quite a lot of antiques, particularly at the old farms where they have all sort of bits in their sheds such as cartwheels with the old wooden spindles and horse harness gear. Those things are becoming more scarce. Big stone toughs, for instance, are worth hundreds of pounds and old milk churns are becoming very sought after. At one Barnoldswick farm they had some old stuff upstairs in one of the cottages next door. They hadn't a clue how much it was worth and they had a real do. One chest of drawers made £300-£400. They'd just been stuck up there with all sorts of rubbish in them.

I like watching programmes like *Antiques Roadshow* but I think some of the prices they come out with are horrendous. No way I could make so much. But then we don't get that class of antiques although we do get nice pieces now and again. There's usually something in every sale.

People will come from all over the place for a farm sale. I had one in February near Sedbergh and there was people ringing up from Wales and all over the place. He had some oldish tackle like Ferguson mowing machines. As soon as the advert appeared I told him he would be very busy on the phone. I always put the farmer's number in the paper and advertise in the *Farmer's Guardian* which is one of the best, as well as the farmer's own local paper.

I don't think auctioneering varies much in different parts of the country. It all depends how you meet your farmers. If you don't get on with your farmers you might as well not be there. You have to have a crack. There's one farmer I ask every time he comes to the auction at ten or half past, 'Have you just got up, Jack?' 'Have I buggery!' he says, 'I've been up hours'. I know he hasn't because he's sixty-something and he has two lads who look after most of the work these days. But he enjoys his leg being pulled a bit. Some of them don't like it but you soon get to know. You're about 45 miles from Skipton to Sedbergh so you see a lot of farmers. It's having the crack with them and enjoying your work – that's what it's all about.

THE ARTIST Katharine Holmes

Artist KATHARINE HOLMES (36) has a comfortable studio in a Dales village but, undeterred by the vagaries of the Yorkshire weather, she is more likely to be found outdoors in the wild remote areas she knows so well. The moors and the fell tops are her work-place and her paintings reflect the dramatic moods of the land-scape around her.

I was born in Malhamdale and came back into the Dales in 1990. I'd been away in the eighties doing my Fine Art degree at Newcastle University and then a further degree. I also worked in various galleries and museums, including Abbot Hall in Kendal, Glasgow's Hunterian Art Gallery and Christchurch Mansion in Ipswich.

While I was in Glasgow I was doing quite a lot of work on the west coast of Scotland but all the time I was away I was coming back and painting the Dales. I'm particularly interested in this area because it's familiar – it's what I know and am emo-tionally attached to. Even if I were to live away again I wouldn't like to think I'd never come back. I always want to maintain a link with people and places here, it's where my roots are.

My grandmother the watercolourist Constance Pearson lived at Malham for many years and I grew up there surrounded by her pictures. She painted outside in all weathers and it always seemed the natural thing to do to be out trying to put down in paint what is happening in the landscape.

I love to travel and spend time both in cities and different landscapes. I went to Japan in May and when I come back from abroad or even from a short trip I'm always amazed by the beauty of the area. With living in and painting the Dales it is easy to become complacent, a bit over-familiar, so sometimes I have to get away. Anyway I like much that cities have to offer and find it very necessary to keep looking at art and listening to what is happening.

Much of my painting is done out of doors. I usually just sit down on the ground with my materials spread all around. Painting outdoors enables me to respond to the atmosphere of the place, to the ever-changing weather and light. I feel that I can only get close to what is happening in the landscape by painting in this way. It's about the experience of being in a place, it's not just about the look of a place. It's about what it feels like to be there at a certain time of the year – often very cold! I very much like the winter – not from the practical paint-ing point of view because it's so cold and windy but because I like the look of it – the sort of bare bones of the landscape. For painting, the height of the summer when everything is very grey and green is not always as interesting.

I tend to work in series making paintings in one particular location sometimes over several years. One of the places where I have done a lot of work and I still keep returning is Boss Moor above Hetton. It has everything – unlimited sky, acres of rough moorland, and long views over pasture and meadow to distant hills.

One of the things I'm very interested in when I paint outside is the weather. The painting is as much about weather as places. Painting from the car isn't the same as being outside. I have to be in the landscape to feel the cold and the light passing over it.

I dress for the weather and sometimes I take a tent to keep the rain off or I dodge the showers by retreating into the back of the car. I do go out in all weathers. I'm responding to what's happen-ing in the environment, in the place and would find it hard to produce some of my paintings in a centrally heated studio.

I'll generally work over two or three days outside on a paint-ing but in January on Boss Moor I might only go out for two or three hours at a time if it's really bad weather. I sometimes have painted when it's been very foggy and people who see me must think 'What on earth is she painting?' Sometimes I've painted when it's been pouring with rain just to see what happens

Previous page: Katharine Holmes works on location, whatever the weather. Here, she is inspired by the awesome landscape at Gordale Scar.
PHOTOS: JERRY HARDMAN-JONES

Right: Katharine in her studio with her painting of Gordale Scar

when the rain soaks the paint off the paper. So I work with what's happening at the time.

Apart from the weather sometimes dictating when I work, I work from deadline to deadline as I have exhibitions planned for months ahead. On a nice day it doesn't feel like work but on bad days you still have to turn out and I find conditions very challenging.

Being an artist can seem a casual sort of job but its still a job and like any, has to be worked at. Some paintings are made quite easily and some aren't. It depends on so many different things, often its the weather conditions.

Currently I'm working a lot in mixed media on handmade paper with watercolours, inks, pastel and collage. I tear sheets of paper and stick them on the main support of the painting. The idea came from the roughness of the terrain.

I like to work experimentally and a lot of what I do is about finding equivalents for the different elements of landscape, whether it is the softness of moorland grass, the transparency of a cool blue sky or the solidity of a limestone cliff.

I also work in oil on canvas at the moment, a series about Gordale Scar, some of which will be exhibited at Leeds University in January 1999. They're almost abstract, to do with the texture and substance of rock and the atmosphere of the place. As well as being interested in things like the nature of the materials and the similarities between the materials and the paints I like to transpose parts of the landscape into the paintings. I started mixing gravel into paint out of curiosity. Then it seemed right to do it so I carried on.

Working with brushes, palette knives and rags I build up craggy and smooth surfaces of oil paint and will then work into these adding further texture with glimmer pigments, natural micas, glass fragments, grass and gravels. Sometimes I will pour thin paint or varnish in an attempt to understand and make a new surface.

I have long been fascinated by the similarities between painted surfaces and rock. Quite often I'll work on a few pictures at a time. I have certain sizes and formats I like to work on which I feel comfortable with and which seem the right scale for both the subject and my studio. I work quite often for several days on one picture. The paintings made outside in watercolour influence the ones made in the studio and vice versa. Both types of work are essential to each other.

Although much of what influences my work comes from direct contact with the landscape as I said earlier I keep looking at the work of other artists past and present.

I suppose Turner is a very obvious choice. I'm very interested in his work, his watercolours in particular. I'm always asking 'How did he do that?' I look at him again and again; I suppose I always will. Just to pick out two other names I'm also influenced by several Scottish artists, Joan Eardley in particular who painted the sea at Catterline in Aberdeenshire. Also more recently, Barbara Rae.

Although I've always known I wanted to paint it took me a long time to work out how to be able to do it full time. I don't know that I've altogether worked it out – it is sometimes a precarious occupation... I am very fortunate however to be doing what I am interested in and to be continuing to sell the paintings I produce both in the Dales and much farther afield.

I've been fortunate really. I'm not making pots of money but I'm ticking over. I'm fortunate in that my work seems to sell. For many artists it doesn't and I don't feel I'm having to compromise at all. I'm lucky that people seem to understand my work and that it's very accessible. It appeals to people not only who like art but who like the places I paint.

Im continually building up contacts with galleries, curators and collectors and enjoy meeting and working with all these people as much as I like to be in the studio or best of all out on the hills!

PHOTOGRAPHERS
Eliza & John Forder

ELIZA (50) and JOHN FORDER (52) have a photographic gallery in the village of Dent. Their books have catalogued the life of people working in the Dales and John specialises in cave photography. Eliza has recently opened a Meditation Centre attracting people from all over the world. Daughter Rachel (32) lives in Spain teaching meditation, Abigail (23) is studying in London and Charlotte (18) is at the University of East Anglia reading ecology.

Eliza: Living in a remote location like Dent means that we are constantly exploring new ways of making a living. It's the only way you can survive here. We do want our photography to go on, since the success with our series of books in the eighties, but these big photographic books were popular then. They were new then and became a fashion. We just happened to be here doing the right thing at the right time with a very supportive publisher and printer behind us. In the nineties, the fashion for these books began to wane and we had to find other ways of earning a living. I think that speaks for many people who live here. You constantly have to find other things to do to keep yourselves going.

John: Working at Whernside Manor, an outdoor pursuits centre at the time, was the start of the photography. I was always keen on taking pictures of caves. I was an instructor in outdoor pursuits with the emphasis on caving. There was a dark room at the Centre and I made a lot of prints in my own time. The photography business started when Whernside Manor closed down and I was made redundant. As soon as any shock like that happens you're immediately forced into a different direction. We once ran up nearly £700 on our credit card on food just in order to survive! But I think the times of financial hardship or pressure push you on. If you have money you wouldn't draw upon your own resources.

The photographic gallery evolved from a junk room and coal shed! We cleared it all out and stuck a few of my caving pictures on the walls and people seemed to like them. We also had some old glass plate negatives of Dent which were very popular with local people. We framed them ourselves and they sold really well. They brought people in and so we decided to put more of our own work on display and that's still on-going.

Eliza: I had always enjoyed photography and had taken photographs of actors and actresses when I lived in London. So we decided to put a story together of the people who live in the Dales, their way of life which had never really been portrayed, and the landscape. It was a question of exploring our different talents and interests plus trying to portray the Dales in a different way, not just as a tourist attraction place with chocolate box pictures but about the life that really went on there.

We knew a few of the subjects before we photographed them and one person led us to another. We got to know them on a completely different level. By going out with them and watching them work, we became far more familiar with the way of life that went on. After we did *Open Fell, Hidden Dale* we then went on to do a complementary book on the Lake District, again, trying to get much deeper into the people who live and work there. We were then given the opportunity to do the book *Hill Shepherd* which was a much more broad sweep of the farming people here in the north west, including Teesdale. It was probably the broadest survey and deepest research that's been done on the life of the hill farmer through photographs and words.

On one occasion in Deepdale we were taking pictures of sheep dipping. For the most part, dipping sheep is done outside but this was happening inside a barn. Often in barns they have gutters on one side and I just thought it was a swill gutter – I never dreamt it would be a sheep dip. I stepped further and further back trying to get a better picture until I fell in, camera and all – John's camera! The camera was fine but the only thing I can remember was John threatening that I'd have to walk back because I smelt so bad.

John: We didn't mind the early hours and the bad weather. We really enjoyed going on sheep gathers high up on to the fells. It was a day's job and they would often start at four in the morning. Eliza would go with one shepherd and I would go with another, each taking a camera, and we would meet up at the top and chivvy the sheep back down.

Eliza: To me that was the highlight. I enjoyed that more than the more detailed work although from the more detailed work, I learned about all the work involved with the sheep. In fact that's why I started eating lamb again! We could see that the sheep were treated well and they're obviously free range.

John: We couldn't carry heavy tripods and big lenses so we each took a medium format camera and a 35mm camera for back up and we used fast film. We didn't use tripods even indoors because in the barns there was always activity and people moving around. We used flash but we had to invent little flash techniques to soften the light – we couldn't transport umbrellas like they use in studios to soften the light because flash can be quite harsh so I made some little bounce cards that we attached to our flash guns. It was makeshift and improvisation just to improve the quality of the photographs.

Eliza: My favourite photographs were ones John took of Ennis (a local farmer) inside her barns. The light was very soft. I loved some of the interior shots. They conveyed the atmosphere that this could have been going on for hundreds and hundreds of years.

I couldn't believe how much went on in the hill farming life that many people just hadn't a clue about. I was aware of lambing time – that's obvious – but apart from that, I didn't know all the different stages or dates, for instance, the time the tup was put to the ewe and when spayning happened and what it was – that's when the mothers are separated from the lambs. That was one of the reasons why we wrote the books. We were determined not to sentimentalise life in the Dales but to keep it in the present and that's why it worked.

John and Eliza Forder outside their home and studio in Dent, a village where they say there is a lively population and a thriving young community

There was a wonderful reaction to the books. People were delighted that suddenly some interest had been paid to their way of life. It wasn't another book on Middleham Castle or woolly lambs gamboling in the fields, it was a realistic look. When we took a picture of the farmer skinning the lamb I remember thinking 'Should we put this one in?' and I thought 'Yes, that's what happens'. People were very surprised by that but they respected the fact that it had to be included.

Producing books is an addictive thing. Once you've done one book, you want to go on and do another and the one thing about living here in the Dales, especially in a place like Dent, is

that so many social changes have gone on in the past 24 years. We have also seen a number of changes in the village itself.

John: We're right in the centre of the village and in the past twenty years there has been a huge increase in heavy vehicles which come through the village and rattle the houses. All deliveries these days seem to happen in big vehicles. Even when we had books delivered there weren't very many but they came in an enormous pantechnicon.

Eliza: The other big difference in the village is the variety of people who live here. You maybe associate a Dales village with retired people and farmers but that's simply not the case in Dent. There's an extremely lively cosmopolitan mixed group of people and a good young community. There are new houses which are relatively cheap and this is encouraging young people to either move here or stay here. The school is bigger now than it's ever been.

After the series of photography books, we then changed emphasis. I'd always been interested in the way the north of Great Britain had inspired or drawn people to it – artists, photographers, people seeking fulfilment in different ways. We had the idea of doing a book exploring all the different ways people found spiritual inspiration from the north. We wanted to make it

an historical book. So we went right back to Celtic spirituality where there was a close relationship with nature, to the early Christians, and we followed the story through taking us right to the poets and artists in the 19th century who were drawn to the north. It was entitled *The Light Within* and was sponsored by the Rowntree Trust. They saw it as a book to inspire people spiritually in a materialistic society.

We were trying to take in a different market and trying to develop our photography in a different way. It was fascinating to do and took us to Iona and Holy Island and to many places we'd never have bothered going otherwise. We also included some caving, climbing and paragliding – outdoor pursuits – because they're all different ways people find inspiration. Nothing like that had been done before and it was very well received.

After *The Light Within* people kept saying 'We want you to go deeper why not write your own story?' so I wrote *In Search of Freedom* which was autobiographical. Meanwhile, John became involved with freelance editorial work.

John: I felt because we were involved with writing that the logical progression might be to do that more professionally. I was very lucky to get work with a local firm of scientific publishers. I work from home which suits me down to the ground. It means I can

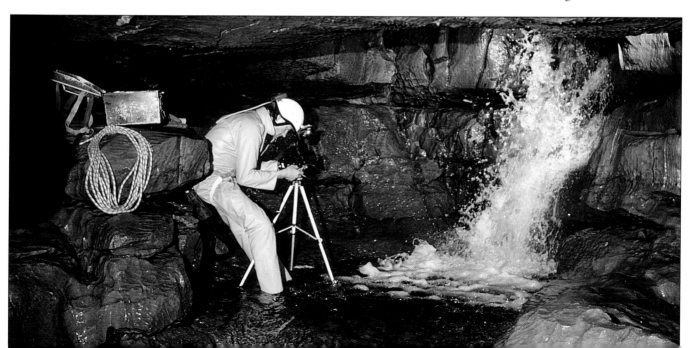

(Opposite) *Photographing at Long Churn*
PHOTO: J & E FORDER

Local farmer, Mrs Lambert, feeding the fowl
PHOTO: J & E FORDER

have a certain amount of freedom. If it's a nice day I can go for a walk as long as I make up for it later at some stage. It doesn't matter to me if I work Saturday and Sunday and have time off during the week. It's better if you're not trying to go to places at the same time as everybody else. I occasionally do 'in house' work which I enjoy but a day or two a month in an office is different from five days a week.

I love it here. I still do caving instructing from time to time but again it's all part and parcel of the variety which is so attractive about being based in a place like this. Not far from here is one of the longest explored cave systems in the world, a very interesting cave with a variety of passages. I decided to do a photography project documenting a through trip from one entrance to the other – which is proving to be problematic! You need helpers who are willing to hang around but I feel the end result will be of interest to cavers.

Our photography always seems to work best if it's focused on a particular topic. It's too easy to take out the camera and think 'That's a good shot, I'll take a snap of that' but afterwards you think 'Why did I bother? What am I going to do with it?' You need a goal to work towards.

John: We both did the research for our books on life in the Dales but Eliza did the writing. It's funny, but people who came into the studio assumed I was the one who had taken all the photographs. I tried to put them right and tell them it had been a joint project but then they would say 'Oh, your wife helps you?' I don't know what they thought she did – load the film for me?

Eliza: I certainly want to carry on with my photography but take it in a different way and maybe do more abstract work. I am currently very much involved with teaching meditation which is something I've done for the over 25 years. It's simply a very beneficial way of releasing the stresses and of modern living. People of all ages and walks of life come to the Centre which was opened this year in the village. Hopefully, that will go from strength to strength.

COTTAGE GARDENER Robin Strange

Robin Strange (51) was born in Oakham in Rutland and moved to Lancashire when he was a year old. He now runs a forestry business from their home at Coniston Cold where they have lived for 27 years. He and wife Anne's summer floral display is a real show-stopper appreciated by everyone travelling on the A65. During the 1998 World Cup, Robin added a notice saying : 'I hate football!' just in case anyone was under the impression that was why he had the England flag flying. Their flag flies proudly every summer – World Cup or not!

We'd been to Switzerland quite a bit and I love the attitude they have over there – very nationalistic. They're very proud of their country and I was getting fed up of the lack of pride in ours.

I'd thought about having a flag for a while but that year was a European Cup year and I hate football so I thought I wouldn't do it while the football was on. I waited until it was over and then tried to buy a flag but it was like trying to get hold of a gold bar. I went all over the place and eventually found one in York. The first day I put it up, a chap had stopped to take some photographs of our flower baskets and he asked why I'd put the flag up. I replied, 'Do you need a reason for putting the flag of your country up?' There's no pride left, it's just gone out of the window. I was amazed somebody had to ask.

The idea for baskets started when we went to York for a day. I was walking through the Shambles and saw the hanging baskets and I've always loved fuchsias. My mother and my aunties all grew them and I thought I must have a go. I always liked gardening but I'd never done container gardening. We just bought stuff in the first year and played around with it – just a few hanging baskets.

To begin with it looked so bland that I thought I could do better so I converted a shed into a greenhouse by replacing the roof with plastic sheeting. We have three greenhouses now and grow everything from seed. Everything you see in the display has been grown by ourselves. The fuchsias are all from this year's cuttings.

We get a lot of east wind which comes straight across and we used to find the baskets horizontal with the plants snapped off. I'd had enough of that so I tried to wire them down but that made it even worse because they couldn't move and they'd break off even more easily. I thought I'd try and see if boxes and containers would be more rigid and that worked.

As well as baskets, we used boxes, mangers, all sorts of things. I've made everything because they're too expensive to buy and being in the forestry business myself I had the raw material. I keep adding stuff and people keep saying that one of these days it's all going to collapse but the wall's three foot thick and it's a 300-year old house so I think we're safe enough!

We turned the house upside down and moved the lounge upstairs. The wall was just high enough to install a 5ft door so I thought I'd have a balcony. I'd always wanted one, the idea again coming from Switzerland – when I build something it's built for a hundred years! I built it to the corner, then built a platform as a separate entity but then I realised I couldn't get across. I was climbing up a ladder to get to the plants so I ended up building the corner piece. That made access a lot easier to plants that were always a pain to dead-head, particularly petunias which you have to practically do on a hourly basis... if you let them go to seed then the plant has done its job. If you don't take the heads off, you don't get any flowers.

I set the seeds off in a professional seed compost which is a very low based fertilizer. A lot of people – my mother did this – buy growbags in bulk because they're cheap but they are very very high in nutrients which is the one thing you do not want for seeds because it burns the very fine roots.

I built an automatic watering system incorporating an automatic feeding system. I line the baskets with traditional moss. I don't use polythene or trays. The secret to this sort of thing is never leaving it, always being on top of it. I look after them like babies really.

The containers usually go outside about the second week in June but that would depend on where in the country you live. I've had trouble with frost and we've lost a lot of dahlias. I grow everything from seed or from cuttings. I don't use tubers because you've got to know when they're going to come up. That's all right in the front garden but when you're doing a display like this, tubers might appear three weeks after all the seeds come have up and they push all the plants out.

Most baskets are kept in the greenhouse but the main display has to be planted up outside on site. We do it over a period of about a month from start to finish.

I make a lot of mistakes but the secret is knowing your plants. I can never remember many of the Latin names but I don't bother with things like that – I'm a true amateur. I look in a seed catalogue and think that looks a nice plant but I don't take any notice of the height then I find it grows ten times higher than anything else and you can't see the things you've planted underneath.

I've never been one for formal gardens. People say ours is a riot of colour and that's really what I like, making it pleasant for myself and other people. I can't do with all this colour coordinating things – they can keep that down in London.

The contrast and variation gives that visual impact. Anne's frightened of heights so she does the lower end and I do the top end. She'll come home from work and get the tea on and then come out and take a few dead heads off while the tea's cooking. Although it's hard work, it's relaxing, very de-stressing. It takes at least a couple of hours a day. It depends on how much time you've got!

The whole display needs watering twice a day whether it's overcast or not, they dry out so fast with the wind. It's a serious error of judgment to think that they don't need watering if it's been raining. If we get really heavy rain, like a thunderstorm, most of the water has run off. If you were to take some of the plants out of the hay manger on the wall, it would be just a mash of roots, a matted mass. It takes as long to take it down and sometimes longer. It's solid and winds itself into everything. I keep nothing for the following year.

I've lost count of the number of containers. People ask me how many plants I use so last year I thought I'd count them

and there were just over 7,500.

My greenhouse is heated so I start taking cuttings in January. I don't keep the main fuchsia plants. I find that they go very woody. You can run them for two or three years but you get fewer and fewer flowers.

I go for things that look different. I try them out in one area and if they don't work, I don't bother with them again.

We used to have electric heating in the greenhouse. One winter, we had 4,500 plants in there and there was a power cut. The family had to get up and take them all into the house. They were all over the floor. Then we had to carry them all back out! It's all gas now which is a lot easier to handle.

You should stuff the baskets full. I hate to see a basket with about four plants in it. Some of mine get a hundred. These baskets which have little squares are absolute rubbish! How can you get a plant in there? It's impossible. People see these on special offer and don't stop to think they're on special offer because they're hopeless! They never get going. Hay manger baskets which are open are far better – or plastic baskets which you can pull apart.

A lot of it is personal trial and error. The secret to taking cuttings is cleanliness. You must sterilise the knife. If you take one cutting and it's diseased, then you take another, you spread the disease.

We have our own compost heap and when we finish at the end of the year, we empty all the stuff into it. I've never done composting properly like they say in the books, I just dump it in and cover it over with some black polythene. You end up with seeds coming up all over – sometimes we have tomatoes growing in the middle of flower displays. But we never put weeds in it – that's fatal. We buy new compost every year for the display. I spend probably £200 on compost every year.

One of the big things is not to rush into it. People see this and say 'I've got to rush back and copy that'. You've got to build it up slowly. I've made loads of mistakes but one of the big things that keeps me going are all the cards people send to 'The house with all the flowers on' or 'The floritious wall, Coniston Cold' – the most weird addresses but they always find me.

A friend helps organise coach tours for Help the Aged. He said did we realise we were on the coach tour now. Apparently when they're coming round the Dales they make a detour!

We had some nice people from America recently. One night it had almost gone dark and there was this great flash. I thought it was lightning but there were a load of Japanese with movie cameras and flashes, all taking pictures.

Robin and Anne Strange with a small section of their display - for lesser mortals, it could easily be a full time job

Sometimes I think I can't be bothered doing it next year, particularly when it's been a summer with bad weather and a lot of wind with things getting damaged and blown about.

I did it for my own pleasure to start with and it's just got massive now. People come to look at the wall, not me! But if it gives people pleasure, that's all that matters.

When we went on holiday my mother used to come and stay and look after the flowers. She treated it as a holiday and loved chatting to everyone who stopped to take pictures. She was so proud of the display. Sadly, she died earlier this year – I lost my biggest fan who gave me inspiration and always gave me encouragement when things went wrong. My display is dedicated to her memory.

HANG GLIDER & PARAGLIDER Liz Addy

Liz Addy (41), an optometrist, was born in Nottingham and brought up in Leeds where she went to school until she was 18. After studying opthalmic optics at college in Glasgow, she later returned to Yorkshire to live near her father.

I've always liked Yorkshire, I've always been a walker and I've always liked the mountains and hills. I've moved from village to village in the area and now I've been in Addingham for fourteen years – the longest time I've lived anywhere.

I first took up paragliding in 1991. I'd always been interested in flying and when I lived in Leeds one of the forefathers of hang gliding world, Bob Bailey, lived near me. Although I'd thought about taking it up, I put the idea on hold as I'd just started my career and was working weekends with only four weeks holiday a year.

In the last few years I became self employed and thought, 'Right, I'm going to do this!' There was a school based at Kilnsey called Northern Paragliding and they then moved to Hawes. The first year I never even went near the place because the weather was always bad but the next year I eventually got going. Ian Currer and Rob Cruickshank from Northern Paragliding are extremely good, they write books on paragliding and do teaching videos and they really encouraged me. I was a complete novice and had never done anything really scary or out of the ordinary.

You start off by doing bunny hops, laying the glider out on the ground and pulling it up into the wind. There's usually just

Liz Addy takes off from Whernside in pursuit of her favourite hobby

Liz with some of her trophies

a slight slope initially so you're maybe only10ft off the ground. Then you get the hang of going higher until eventually you have the skills to be safe and take on something a bit bigger. When you're doing your first soaring flight it's absolutely wonderful. There's only wind noise and it's very peaceful.

What I like best about it is being high up which is why I like climbing as well. When I'm stood on a mountain looking down I get the same feeling as when I'm the air – the sheep and cows and fields are tiny and I love the sensation when you're above all the hills. It's a totally different perspective.

For your first few days' training you use equipment belonging to the school then when you start getting to the soaring stage, you're better off getting your own equipment because you get used to it. It's better to have the experience on the same gear and by that time you've decided you want to take up the sport. You should buy a glider according to your experience. People often buy paragliders which are too advanced for them and get into predicaments.

A paraglider looks like a rectangular parachute but it flies like a glider. The harness is like a chair so you're sitting in a very comfortable position. A hang glider is like a kite with an A-frame control and you're dangling in there. The flying through the air is the same but it's a different machine and the way you handle the machine is different.

You can steer a paraglider, it's not like a parachute where you just drop out of an aeroplane and drift with the wind. You have control over where you're going to go. It's very manoeuvrable, just two controls like toggles in each hand and you just pull the right one to go right and vice versa although it's not quite as simple as that! Especially when you're beginning, your canopies are quite small and you've got small harnesses so it's not an awful lot of weight to carry up and down the hill – it's a different kettle of fish with hang gliders.

My first flying was all done in the Dales but I went seeking bigger mountains. Not necessarily just to take off and fly to the bottom but because the weather sometimes is bad here and also I'm a traveller. In my first year of flying, I went to Israel with the school and flew off cliffs in various Israeli resorts. We flew off a hill overlooking Nazareth and also one near Galilee. Then I went out to the Alps and flew wearing skis, taking off and landing on snow. I've flown in India in Goa, and in Nepal I've flown off a mountain at 19,000 ft. Sometimes in countries like Nepal you're actually flying with the choucas, eagles, buzzards and ravens and you find the air currents just like they do. It's a really fantastic feeling.

I've also flown in most of the European countries – France, Spain, Portugal, Germany, Austria and I've been to Romania this year. Nearer home, I also fly in the Lake District, Dales and Scotland.

The hill you will go to depends on the wind directions. The weather is so fickle. It could be north westerly one day and south easterly another day. Most of my training flights were around Hawes, Semerwater, Wether Fell, Dodd Fell and Kirkby Stephen. You start off flying from near the bottom of the hills then as you get better and you learn how to soar you can take off from the top of the hill and using the air currents soar at 500 ft or so. Eventually you start to look for thermals so you can climb even higher and eventually think about going cross-country. That is really satisfying when you've actually gone somewhere with no engine, using your own skill. You can fly a hundred miles – if you're as good as that. I suppose one of my best flights was from Grove Head which is near Wether Fell. I took off from there and flew about 18 kilometers and landed near Kettlewell in a field, which was great! I should have gone in a slightly different direction because I reckon I'd have gone a lot further.

The paraglider packs up into a rucksack and when you're learning you've got the really basic stuff which is quite lightweight, probably about 10 kilos. But when you go in for competition flying you end up with a camera and radio and an instrument called a vario with an altimeter which tells you whether you're going up or down and what height you're at. When you've got all this kit together you can have a bag, similar to a rucksack, weighing about 15-18 kilos. If you've flown cross-country, you put it on your back and walk to the nearest road and hitch a lift back. As there aren't so many paraglider or hang glider pilots around, most people are very helpful and willing to give you a lift. If they're tourists then you can tell them a little bit about the area and point out places of interest and show them other people flying. They think that's wonderful because they wouldn't otherwise have had that opportunity.

I'm in the Dales Hang Gliding and Paragliding Club. There are about 300-400 members although they don't all live in the Dales. Some might fly in the Dales only once a year when they come up for a holiday but we have quite a strong group of local fliers from Hawes, Middleham, Leyburn, Ripon and further north east towards Newcastle as well as a lot of people from Leeds and Bradford.

From a safety point of view, you try to always fly with somebody or at least be on the hill with somebody else, even a walker, in case of accidents. If there are a lot of you together on the hill then it's brilliant, it's a good social gathering. The sport is as safe as you make it. It is inherently dangerous because at altitude things can go wrong. You have to make the right decisions. You can't just freeze, you have to think calmly and logically and you have to watch the weather. But if you're careful and you make sensible assessments, you can minimise the risk.

Take-offs and landings are often the most dangerous times - when you're close to the ground. If it's a steep rocky slope or if there's a strong wind, it can be tricky. So can landing in a place you're not familiar with such as when you have flown cross-country.

I've been frightened a few times, particularly in the stronger conditions abroad. In Spain, for instance, the thermals get very powerful. If it's becoming stormy then you really need to be on the ground. It can cause your canopy to collapse and if you hit turbulence it can do erratic things. It's better to avoid flying in those conditions. You should be watching for those all the time and land before it becomes dangerous but sometimes it happens more quickly than you expect. We do have a reserve parachute but I've never had to use it and I don't want to!

Paragliders can fly 40 kilometers an hour whereas the high performance hang gliders can go a lot faster, 100 kilometers an hour in theory. I'd been hankering to learn hang gliding as well but I didn't really get going until last year and had to finish off my training in France because the weather was so bad here.

The hang glider is heavier than the paraglider although mine is quite light, 25 kilos. When you're learning and you're doing little bunny hops just like you do on the paragliding, you're having to go up and down the hill many times and it's really hard work which is why women tend to fly paragliders rather than hang gliders. Apart from that, once you've mastered the technique, there's no reason why a woman can't fly a hang glider or paraglider just as well as a man. I must admit I was struggling recently carrying up the hill and actually asked someone to help me but then a friend of mine also needed help to carry his glider. Everybody helps each other.

There are lots of local and national competitions which I find help my flying. It usually pushes you a bit further than you would do normally. I've been to Portugal flying three times and was third in the competition and also the first woman. I also have the Portuguese Ladies' Distance record for flying the furthest. The next year I was first woman again but not so high up in the competition. Our team of four also won a competition in Spain. We have a local club competition called the Baildon Sod on Baildon Moor. It's just a glide competition and started in the old days when people didn't really know how to build, fly and make hang gliders. They could fly to the moon before they could fly hang gliders! Leonardo had drawn one but he didn't actually have the materials to build it with. If he had had our modern lightweight materials, his design would have flown.

Flying a plane with an engine does appeal to me but not so much in this country because there's an awful lot of having to talk to air traffic control. At the moment hang gliding is free flying. You take off from a site you have agreed with farmers and that's very important to mention – we do get permission from farmers and it's through the goodwill of farmers that we're able to fly.

I'm having a lot of fun with the hang gliding but I still have a long way to go, it's still a learning curve. I could be tempted to take up microlighting which is really like a hang glider with an engine on it. I'd love to fly on the plains of Africa..

David Gallivan at Illusion Pot, Kingsdale. The Cave Rescue
Organisation, based at Clapham, covers the Three Peaks area of the
Yorkshire Dales, into Cumbria and the Kirkby Lonsdale area, across to
Malham and down to the borders of Bowland
PHOTO: H LIMBERT

CAVE RESCUER Dave Gallivan

Dave Gallivan (49) runs a climbing, walking and caving company known as Yorkshire Dales Guides and has been associated with the Cave Rescue Organisation for over thirty years. His wife Margaret is a senior radiographer for General Services and is a PACS trainer, at Leeds General Infirmary. Elder son Michael (17) is in his final year at Settle community college and John (15) attends Settle High School.

I was born just outside Leeds and ever since I was 14 I've had a fascination with the Dales. My friend and I used to hitchhike up to Horton-in-Ribblesdale to go camping at Beecroft Hall. We progressed from there to caving and even managed a few caving trips abroad but we always said that one day we were going to work in the Dales.

After a short interval abroad in Canada and Australia I was offered a job with ICI at the quarry in Horton and then Tarmac took it over. It was shortly after that that I decided my future was best elsewhere. Because you have so few options for employment in the Dales and the majority of people work for themselves, I decided to become self employed in 1992 and form a little company called Yorkshire Dales Guides, taking groups climbing, walking and caving. I'd done part time work before for various organisations and I decided it was time to do it myself on a freelance basis.

I was fortunate early on to get some work with Lancashire County Council and North Yorkshire. The benefit of me being freelance was that was that my wife Margaret could work full time. So for a short time I was a house husband – I often wonder if I was the first house husband in the Dales. While the business was building up and there was only a small number of groups, it meant that I was at home more than I was out working but the kids were at school so it worked out rather well. Once they were older and could look after themselves, I was

able to progress further and work longer hours.

A typical day depends on the time of year. Winter is the time you don't go to the pub because you can't afford it and Summer's the time you'd like to go to the pub but you haven't got the time. For instance, tomorrow I have a group on the Adventure Trail which is like an outdoor Crystal Maze. This is always popular as it involves team challenges with some simple climbing and caving as well as lots of problems to solve.

Other days I could be taking people walking and teaching navigational skills or introducing novices to the wonders of the underground or visiting a classic cave system with the more experienced caver. I also work with groups on residentials looking at team work and leadership skills as well as conservation work. This year I worked with groups of underachieving young people building an orienteering course at Gisburn Forsest. We designed it for groups of all ages and abilities.

When the groups arrive in the village, I meet them in the car park. I've heard leaders announcing to the kids: 'There, look at Malham Cove' as they point towards the quarry. I'm always amazed about how naive people are about the Dales. You get a lot of people who are apprehensive about walking through villages at night time because of the lack of lighting and there are others who might have seen a sheep or cow for the first time. It's amazing how closeted the youth of today can be. Their usual scenario is school, home, then playing on computers.

No matter how many times you brief the people who are bringing groups, some still come in unsuitable gear. I had to send one lot back because they turned up in high heeled shoes and light suits.

There's a huge diversity of ages – the youngest I take is about nine or ten and the oldest is about 73. The balance is still probably more male than female but girls are far superior to boys. They'll always have a go but the boys are more hesitant because they don't want to make fools of themselves. I'm always impressed by young people, there's too many people knocking them these days.

My involvement with the Cave Rescue Organisation started many years ago as a young lad. All members of Cave Rescue no matter where they are in the country work on a voluntary basis. In my early days there was a rescue at Mossdale Caverns which was probably one of the biggest rescues this country has seen and I hope we never see one like it again.

The weather forecast had been totally wrong. It was a warm, balmy day. Six young university people had been working down there trying to extend the caves when they were hit by a sudden downpour. They were missing presumed trapped by flood water but unfortunately they were drowned. That search went on for days and the bodies were never recovered. It was too dangerous to carry on. I've twice been in charge of a rescue where it's had to be called off because you know the people you are looking for are dead and you can't risk the life of a live person in the recovery.

When the cave rescue team was founded in 1935, it was purely for rescuing from caves but now we do more surface incidents with climbers and walkers. We were the first cave rescue team in the world to be formed so we are known as the Cave Rescue Organisation. After that the other areas were known by their area names. We have our main depot at Clapham and a sub station at Malham. We cover the Three Peaks area of the Yorkshire Dales going into Cumbria and the Kirkby Lonsdale area, across to Malham and down to the borders of Bowland.

Round here, we have the longest cave system in the British Isles (52k) and approximately 980 caves. By the end of the year we'll have had around seventy incidents. Because of the way caving has progressed, for example the materials people are wearing and the kit they're using, there are fewer accidents than there used to be. When I first started you needed about ten people to get to the bottom of a cave. Now you can do it with about two. Another advantage is that we now carry pagers and can respond more quickly. All our members are trained in MRC First Aid which is a casualty care qualification. Lower limb injuries are the most common injury. People break their legs walking across boggy ground and falls often result in sprained ankles. Medically, we see cases of heart attacks, angina and asthma.

I'm one of six duty controllers and we take it in turns to be on call seven days a week. We have a Blue and a Red Team both approximately 21 people strong so you're talking fifty or sixty people in total including a support team. The Red Team and Blue Team take it in turns, giving an opportunity for all our team members to gain experience. We're very fortunate here that the police are very wise – we work under their umbrella and always keep them informed but they allow us to get on with the job and leave decisions to our discretion. Because of the area we cover we work for the Lancashire, Cumbria and Yorkshire police.

There have been about four occasions when I've personally been annoyed. There are more and more incidences above ground where people think because of mobile phones they can ring up three nines and we'll come and assist them off the fell. One example was on Ingleborough when we were looking for three young lads. We found two but one was still missing. We kept looking for him – by this time it was about half past four in the morning – until we discovered somebody had given him a lift back to Leeds and he was sitting at home.

I've been involved in rescuing one particular guy twice. On the second occasion his reaction was, 'Oh, not you again!' as we carried him down to the waiting ambulance. His leather jacket and some of his gear was accidentally left behind at our depot. About two days later he rang me to ask if I would send it to him. I went down to the post office in Settle, bought a special parcel box and posted it all. It cost me about £7 and I didn't even get a thank you. So I thought next time he comes up it won't be third time lucky!

On one occasion we had just come off the hill after recovering an eleven-year old body from Gaping Gill. My pager went off to ring Skipton Police Station and they'd had information to say that a father had rung up to tell them his little boy was missing on Ingleborough. When we asked him when he'd last seen the lad he replied, 'The top of Ingleborough'. He hadn't realised he was missing until they reached Newby. I said, 'Well, that's a fair way that, isn't it?' and his excuse was that his daughter was playing up so he hadn't really noticed his son was no longer with them.

I thought where the heck do I begin to search. I asked him, 'Did you go up the same way you came down?' 'No.' 'Do you think your son saw you setting off on this footpath down the fell?' 'Oh, I'm sure he did,' the father said, then added, 'You'll have no trouble finding him because he's wearing all the modern kit in red and yellow so he'll stand out like anything. That's why we bought it for him.' So I couldn't help pointing out, 'Well, you lost him!'

We went out to look for him and we were all hoping he hadn't fallen down a pothole but luckily, he'd been picked up by a farmer on the fell and taken down to the Cave Rescue Headquarters at Clapham. They radioed through to tell us and about ten minutes later there was another message saying, 'His father's just arrived to collect him, I can see him getting out of his car... Oh, he's slapped the kid and bundled him into the car!' And that was the last we saw of them.

Some people tend to lose all form of commonsense. I remember being woken at 2 o'clock in the morning by the local policewoman to say she'd been driving down the road from Ribblehead and thought she'd heard shouts for help and seen the flickering of a fire in the distance. Sure enough, just outside Horton you could hear these occasional shouts for help and could see the glow of a fire. My concern was they were so close to the road, they must be desperate and be badly injured. It was a cold, dark, horrible night and as I approached the shouts got louder and the fire got bigger – there were sparks all over the shop.

When I reached them there was a man with his wife and daughter. The mother was in shorts and a T-shirt and the daughter was wearing baggy tracksuit bottoms. They'd been swopping shorts and trousers to keep warm. They'd done the Three Peaks and weren't sure where they were. I asked them why they didn't have a map and they told me when they realised they were lost, they'd burned the map to light the fire to keep warm. When I asked them where they'd got all the wood, the father told me proudly that he was in the process of smashing up a second farm gate.

The only injury was a cut on the mother's eye. When they'd got the fire going on the ground they'd put some of it on the wall top and hadn't realise it would crack the limestone. As she was speaking, it must have been time for the trouser change because the daughter automatically took her trousers off and the mother started to take her shorts down so they could swop again. When I asked them where their car was they told me, 'Leeds'. They'd come by train and arranged to ring his brother to come and pick them up when they were ready. Unfortunately he lived in Bradford and the husband told me that by that time he would be in bed, drunk as a lord. In the end we took them to Settle Police Station to spend the night.

The bad calls come about 3 o'clock in the morning. Sometimes people tend to leave it too late because they don't want to bother us but we would rather be informed early than later. What we don't record is how many times the Duty Controller gets phone calls from people who are concerned about friends or relatives who haven't turned up but it's often

David and Margaret Gallivan pictured at a family wedding

because they haven't allowed enough time. It can take a good eight to twelve hours to do the Three Peaks. But that's not a problem. The basic rule is if you think you need us, call us. We would prefer to be called out on a wild goose chase than called out when it's too late.

It would make our life easier if every person who went caving or walking left an indication, with someone they could trust, of their proposed route be it on the surface or underground and the time they're expected back.

A lot of people think we're just here to assist climbers, walkers and cavers (crag rats as they're called) who come to the Dales but quite a few times we're called out to assist the local community. Last time was to an old man who was in a home at Settle. He had decided to walk to a farm he used to work at as a lad but managed to get himself lost. We spent all night looking for him and at first light we decided to bring in an RAF Sea King helicopter. Unfortunately, it landed at Settle School at about quarter to six, so we do apologise to all the residents who didn't intend to get up that early! We continued our search and the old man was picked up just past Settle bypass at the side of the River Ribble. He was fully clothed bar he'd lost a shoe and a sock.

An ambulance was sent for and after the paramedics had a look at him he was taken by helicopter to Airedale hospital. Apparently now if you go to the centre where he lives you get accosted by this man sat in the corner asking people if they've heard his story. He doesn't remember how or why but it was nice to get a lift in a helicopter and have they seen his other shoe?

My worst rescue was when I decided after a time that the person we were looking for underground, a man in his twenties, had drowned and that there was no chance of recovering him because of the prevailing weather conditions. We would have been putting our own members' lives at risk. Unfortunately, his wife was at the scene and I was asked if I would go and explain to her why we were going to curtail the rescue until the following morning. She looked at me and said, 'We've only been married for two weeks.'

The following day we went down the cave and after what seemed an eternity I heard on my radio, 'We've found the casualty'. For a moment, I thought that meant the guy was alive

and my heart missed a beat. But unfortunately, he had been had been drowned. That was a very traumatic incident.

This month the team has purchased its third new LandRover which means we are secure for the next twenty years but we need ongoing contributions all the time. We have to pay rates and replace our equipment at the Clapham depot and that costs about £15,000 a year. We have a main fund-raising event at the Broughton Game Show which we share with Wharfedale. That brings us in most of our money and we get a small amount from the Mountain Rescue Organisation.

About 95 percent of people who are rescued will give some form of donation or at the very least a letter of appreciation. The other 5 percent think the work of the rescue service is their entitlement. But I wouldn't like to see schemes such as compulsory insurance. Every rescue team is based on volunteers with a walking or caving background and they don't want to see their fellow walkers bogged down with red tape. The danger if you start going down that road is that when you respond to somebody who has fallen or had an accident the first question wouldn't be 'Where does it hurt?' but 'How much have you got in your pocket?' or 'Where's your insurance?'

Any member of any rescue team would say that what they lose in money they gain in life experience. Sometimes you can walk away from an exhausting rescue and think why the hell were we called out to that? But you can be called out again and because of the team's input that person is alive today. It's always a team effort and it's all worthwhile giving up your time. There's no greater feeling than to walk away from a successful rescue.

I was listening to a chap once speaking about cavers and walkers and I remember thinking, I wish I'd said that. His words were: 'What people don't understand about the Dales is that there is a beauty above ground for those who want to see it but there is also a greater beauty underground for those who want to venture there'.

For further information about Yorkshire Dales Guides tel: 01729 860357
To make a donation to the Cave Rescue Organisation, write to them at Clapham, via Lancaster LA2 8HH

COUNTRY VET Richard Sutcliffe

Richard Sutcliffe (33) is a partner in Bishopton Veterinary Group based in Ripon. His wife, Catherine, is a vet at the same practice which treats both small animals and farm stock in the Upper and Lower Nidderdale areas. A six-part television programme Country Vets *was filmed in and around the practice and screened in February 1998.*

I'm from just outside Harrogate, my parents are farmers and my father is a client of the practice. I was brought up in Harrogate and went to comprehensive school there, then to Edinburgh University for six years. I worked initially in York for two and a half years at a large practice then afterwards in Northumberland for eighteen months with suckler beef and horses. I then moved back down here to the home ground where I saw practice as a student.

The new premises on the outskirts of Ripon were built in 1993. I moved here later that year and became a partner two years ago. We're about 60 percent large animals and 40 percent small. We have a certain amount of horse work and quite a large proportion of pig work as well but the bulk of the practice is dairy and suckler beef, mainly dairy. We have three pig vets, four large animal vets, four small animal vets and around 16,000 small animals under our care.

As a general rule, we cover farms for about twenty miles in any direction, from Masham to Killinghall and just to the other side of Pateley Bridge over to Boroughbridge.

Nearly all my time is spent out of the surgery. I much prefer that. I enjoy seeing people I know and get on well with. I do the bulk of all the horse work that comes into the surgery and I really enjoy that but I would hate to give up the cattle work. I enjoy having a crack with the farmers. There's a lot of leg-pulling goes on. I couldn't work in a urban practice and I couldn't work in an abattoir. These are the two things I just wouldn't want to do.

Otter, my Border Terrier, goes everywhere with me. I actually delivered him for a client in York. I was called to the whelping early one morning and he had his head stuck. I pulled him out and ended up buying him later on. He's nearly ten years old now and a little bit grey. He spends most of his day in the car with me but he seems to enjoy it. He certainly dislikes being left behind when it's too hot for him in the summer.

There's no such thing as a typical week but I start in the morning about half past eight. Whoever's been on call the previous night phones the large animal vets at home and tells us what calls we've got which have come in overnight and what calls we've got which have been pre-arranged. If we need any more drugs to go to the calls, then we call at the surgery otherwise we go straight on and do the calls from home and pick up more calls as and when we've done the ones that we've got. Mrs Brown on reception will ring us with any calls if she thinks we're in the area. All our large animal vets have mobile phones. Lunch is often a question of grabbing something from a shop as I drive past – a sandwich and a bag of crisps – and just carrying on until the work is done.

I was grinding a horse's teeth down earlier on today with a little DIY grinder. It had lost one of its lower teeth and the top tooth was growing down and damaging its gum. It's nasty when you grind your finger as well. That was this morning's bit of excitement! Earlier this week I took a tumour off a cow's tail which was about the size of a melon – that was quite interesting.

It's a very satisfying job. You're helping people all the time but there's the long hours, being on call at night and not getting home until 8 o'clock in the evening when you're not on call. I'm married to one of the other vets in the practice and Catherine and I both do one night each on first call and one night each on second call, two weekends in eight and two half weekends in eight as well.

Bad weather conditions don't bother me – you just put on an extra jumper in the morning! It is cold when you're calving cows and you're stripped to the waist in the driving rain. I did once have to do a Caesarean on a cow on the moor in Northumberland at 2 o'clock in the morning in sub-zero temperatures. I was there for a couple of hours with very little on - working by tractor light, of course. That was a bit of a test of endurance.

I had a finger chewed by a horse last week but I've never had any major injuries. A lot of the injuries you have are self induced. My powers of self preservation have been more finely tuned. Half the time your reflexes save you and you develop a sixth sense for knowing when an animal's going to kick or misbehave or looking like it might bite you. I'm certainly more alert than most owners are as to how the dog's going to react. With cattle, nine times out of ten you get some sort of warning if they're going to kick or jump. When you're treating cats, you can't really wear gloves. We tend to get a good nurse to hold them! If you get really wild farm cats and they haven't been handled at all, you can put them in a crush cage and give them some sedative or take them by the scruff of the neck and hold them at arm's length until they calm down.

By far the most difficult aspect of the job is having to put animals to sleep. The worst thing I've had to do was put a guide dog to sleep which had been a loyal and trusted servant. I found that very, very difficult. At night I have to do everything that comes my way so inevitably some of these are dogs which have to be put to sleep.

On the other hand, surgical cases are always very satisfying. You've had a pretty good idea what you wanted to do and once it's done, it's instantaneous whereas with medical cases you're treating with drugs and you have to see four or five days later whether the drugs have worked.

Animals have far more tolerance to pain than humans. Certainly cattle do. Horses aren't anything like as tolerant as cattle to pain. It's quite incredible how resilient cows are. Things that would put a human in bed for a fortnight, cows just shrug off and look normal the following day. That can be a problem because you have to make allowances for the fact that they can be hiding quite major internal disasters. Peritonitis can mean that they just don't want to eat whereas we would be rolling in agony. It's partly their survival instinct. If they show to predators that they're ill, then they'd be picked off straight away so they've evolved to be resilient.

You come across surprising cases all the time. On a farm I went to this morning, one of his calves had died and I really couldn't believe it because it didn't look that ill at all yesterday. The farmer had given them a late look before he went to bed for the night and they looked fine and seemed to be improving but when he came to them in the morning one was dead. I once had a dog that died under anesthetic and I found that very difficult to cope with. It belonged to a friend of mine as well and I felt absolutely dreadful.

At other times, animals survive against the odds. I went to see a dairy cow which had really severe acute onset mastitis. She was very sick, flat out and couldn't lift her head up. I treated her with the usual drugs that we use to treat mastitis and gave her twenty litres of intravenous fluids. When I went back about lunchtime she'd rallied a bit and I gave her another twenty litres. By night she was stood up eating and looking pretty much normal. Inside twelve hours that cow had gone from complete death to being well on the way to recovery. I was amazed but the farmer was even more amazed. Things like that make your reputation on farms.

It was almost as good as treating a milk fever where you give calcium and they go from literally being on death's door within two or three minutes to being a normal cow again. That is really impressive. I had one of those last night. They'd taken the cow into the milking parlour and she'd slipped on the concrete and couldn't get up. The fact that she'd gone into the milking parlour meant she'd let her milk down and that was enough to stress her and send her down with milk fever. After a dose of calcium she was up within five minutes and walked out. There are very few occasions except in surgical cases where you do see things working as quickly as that.

We have a very modern, well-run small animal practice. There are thirty employees altogether including a practice manager, nurses, dispensers, reception staff, accounts staff and typists. A few job share which makes the whole thing more flexible. A lot of schoolchildren come in to work here – they have to if they want to go to vet school.

If I hadn't become a vet, I'm quite mechanically minded so I probably would have become an engineer. I like fixing things, be it animals or machinery. I used to be very fond of horse riding when I was younger but it was only ever an interest. I don't think I would have made a career out of it but I'd like to start riding again, to get back to some serious competition work. As a child I did a lot of competing, dressage, eventing and tetrathlon. After I qualified as a vet, I started riding in a few point to points. That was very exciting and I enjoyed it but it

Richard Sutcliffe with Otter, his faithful 10-year old terrier who likes to accompany the vet on his rounds

was a bit too hazardous. I had a nasty fall and an overnight stay in hospital and a couple of days off work. My employers weren't too enthusiastic about my continuing my racing career after that so I packed it in.

While Catherine and I were away on honeymoon in July '97, Yorkshire Television approached the practice to make a fly-on-the-wall type documentary. When we came back it was fait accompli, it had all been organised. They started filming about three weeks later and it was shown in February 1998.

They focused on us as a couple because we were newly married and that was an extra point of interest. They would come round with me when I was on duty and in the evening they took us out to the pub and filmed us in the pub. You got used to the cameras after a while. The crew were with us for six weeks to film six half hour episodes. They came to our Christmas party last year and brought the out takes with them.

Before the filming, our trousers were really shabby so we went to the Rohan shop to buy some new ones and joked that we wanted some discount because they were going to be advertised on television. They suggested we contact head office. Catherine sent them a fax the following day and within five minutes they were back on the phone and said get yourselves to the York shop and we'll kit you out. We got a full change of clothes and later appeared in their Spring catalogue. We did a day's modelling for them which was quite amusing.

Catherine and I try not to take our work home but inevitably there's an awful lot of shop talked round the breakfast table. On weekends off we often have people phoning us up or turning up at the door asking for advice or treatment. It's not the sort of job where you can expect to be off duty completely and walk away from it. We live and breathe the job which is one of its redeeming features. I don't mind it unduly – I quite enjoy a sense of feeling of being indispensable, I suppose!

COMPUTER EXPERTS Simon Fern Philip Barlow

SIMON FERN (39) of Thorpe and PHILIP BARLOW (31) of Otley head computer firm Daelnet, the first Website to give information about the Yorkshire Dales. The firm is an Internet Services company offering: Internet access, Website design, Website hosting and total management of Internet projects. The Daelnet offices are in converted farm buildings near Rylstone, Skipton.

Philip: I'm from Hull and went to university at Leeds to do Applied Zoology. I met Simon when he was also studying at Leeds doing Librarianship and later Information Science. I didn't know what to do when I graduated so I decided to come over to Skipton where Simon was involved with a band. Initially, I helped with the many backstage tasks and sound engineering, but I then became a musician in the band and ended up settling here in the Dales.

Simon : We built the first Daelnet site in my living room with a 386 computer we shared between us, squinting at a 14 inch monitor.

Philip: Simon was the initial drive for the idea in the early nineties. About five of us were discussing possible projects but we weren't even considering trading at that point.

Simon: The first thing we thought about trading was kiddies' software and we ended up doing a data base for children. They could dress teddy bears, create fairy stories and search to see whether a fairy story had a fairy godmother in it, for instance, or how many teddy bears were wearing pink trousers. We also did a CD called Patch the Puppy for an educational publisher, another kiddies' software company, with Phil co-writing the music and organising the sound effects with digital synthesisers.

That was a very experimental phase bringing in a lot of people who were all living locally. I then got a Net connection through the BBC Networking club. I'd worked on on-line systems at college so I thought we should be doing things on the Internet. When a *Dales '95* newspaper from the National Park came through the post I suddenly realised the concept of Dales news and information would make a great web site so we decided to build one!

Nobody else had done a site dedicated to the Yorkshire Dales and we were quite chuffed about being the first in the world to put the Dales on the Internet. At first we stuck some graphics in and put one sentence on it 'Welcome to the first Website in the world dedicated to the Yorkshire Dales' and gradually added to it.

One of the guys who was with us at the time, Steve, knew somebody who was involved with Embsay Cricket Club. They gave us a cricket club newsletter so we stuck that on, then we got one from Settle Orchestral Society, then the Red Lion at Burnsall asked us what we thought a pub would do on the Internet. We suspected it would be pretty good so we built a site for the Red Lion and a freebie for Craven College and by then we had a reasonable amount of content.

There was a link on the home page called 'The Planning Office', which went to the pub Website we had created and when you clicked on 'Contact Us' an E-mail program fired up so people could send us E-mails.

We still did all this on this little 'box' in my living room. Then we wanted to offer Internet access because we thought that was the sensible way of getting people in the Dales understanding what it was all about. We looked into setting it up telephone lines, modem racks, computers, fast fibre optics into the Dales. Every time we looked at prices we were just adding zeros to the end and the costs were just ridiculous. We needed 1,000 initial subscribers even to remotely pay off the hardware, never mind the software and so it just wasn't feasible. We had to go back to the drawing board.

About January '96 I spent a couple of days trawling the Internet for every single provider in the United Kingdom who at the time was using an 0345 number (BT Lo-call) to access the Internet.

I found one or two providers that looked very trendy and then I came across the name Zetnet which I remembered having read about in a New Scientist article about a year previously. They had set something up in the Shetland Islands and you don't get much more remote than that! I decided they must know all about Internet access in rural areas so I gave them a ring. Just by pure luck, they happened to be visiting Manchester that week so they called up to where I lived in Thorpe.

They told us we could use their modem racks and we could provide all the Web-based services and E-mail services and use their place as a dial-in point. They had gone national by this point and it was an 0345 number so all our subscribers in the dales could have local call access. Great! So that's what we did and what we're still doing.

Philip: It was time to bite the bullet and buy fifty accounts which meant we were putting our money where our mouth was – we then had to sell fifty accounts. We sold a group of five or six accounts the first week then another three or four the following week and then more and more people became interested and wanted their pages on the Web.

Simon: This was still based at my house and Phil was driving 'into work' by coming up to my house. We had one room blocked off – no kids were allowed – and by then we'd bought a bit more kit. Philip also had a base at his own home and when he was there we were running the business by E-mail between the two of us and our colleagues Steve, James and Tony, who were based in their own homes.

But the main contact point for the public was my home phone which was ringing all day. We had to decide what we were going to do about this and one night we were down in the Red Lion when Liz, the landlady, told us of a local farm where they had converted some unused farm buildings into offices and we should go and have a look. They showed us this room and we loved it. It was perfect.

Philip: We've been in these premises since September '96. When we first moved in we were a partnership trading as

Simon Fern seated at one of the Daelnet computers, discusses a technical point with Philip Barlow

Daelnet but called the Quantum Dot Knowledge Partnership. We called the company Quantum Dot when we were looking for a smart alec name to promote kiddies' games.

Simon: A Quantum Dot is a term in semi conductor research where you have this non-dimensional point in space and time and you use it as storage unit so you can store billion of bytes in a tiny little space.

I was also looking into the idea of what new industries were taking place in the United States and I stumbled across this term Knowledge Company. The idea that companies can now sell a new commodity – knowledge – captured my imagination.

Philip: Having Quantum Dot Knowledge behind us allowed us a couple of facets. Our Web pages have 'Webcraft by Quantum Dot Knowledge'. That allowed us to have our design operation under Quantum Dot Knowledge and our Internet Access operation under the name Daelnet. We feel it gives us a larger corporate feel behind it.

In May last year (1997) – just to confuse matters! – we set up a limited company called QDK Ltd and kept the partnership on but changed the name of the partnership so we're partners in Daelnet but we're co-directors in QDK Ltd. The first for local activities and the second for global and corporate customers.

Simon: The Daelnet Website has got busier and the directory now includes things like food, drink, accommodation, local shops, holidays, places to visit and so on. It's become a lot more comprehensive in terms of what's going on in the Dales. There is a What's New? page for the latest updates as well as North Country Focus which is a news site addressing conservation and countryside issues. We also have numerous sites containing photographs of the Dales in the past. In fact, a whole pile of interesting material about the dales!!

Philip: Our roles are complementary. We're both multifunctional and at the moment we're building a new team who are taking over more of the admin and technical support functions. We've also taken on work experience people and we've been lucky that the ones we've had have paid off, including a 15-year-old.

I'm tied up mainly with designing Websites. Technical graphics is a large part of it. I don't do much original illustration although I feel I could move into that. There's also a lot of coding which is the other side of Web design. You have to produce a page of code which can be interpreted by the browser software which results in a graphical page. People use different computers with different resolutions, different numbers of colours on their display and different fonts on their systems so all these things have to be taken into consideration to make sure your page is displayable on as many computers as possible.

Simon: New technology is infinitely more complex now than it was when we first started. Now you have to understand data structures and Phil has been doing this but increasingly our roles in the technical sense are meeting. It might be me who comes up with the idea of a particular Website then it's up to Phil to work out the best ways to display that content in the most useable manner. Then Phil may need a particular computer to do a particular job and it will be me who will look at the technical side of that and configure the computer to behave how he wants it to behave.

Philip: It isn't a problem having our office in a rural location. What is important is that we both have experience of cities. I grew up in a city and Simon lived for five years in Windsor in Canada. That gives you the power to live rurally yet understand what makes the city tick. City people might come up here and try to be overpowering but it doesn't work on us because we've been there and done that!

When the business ideas came along there wasn't really any decision to be made about where it should be based. We were

both settled here and it never crossed our minds that living here would be a drawback with that sort of business.

Simon: I made the decision that I wanted to stay here when I was at college. I'm not a pure blooded local but my grandfather was a signalman on the Settle Carlisle line based at Horton-in-Ribblesdale and my mother was born up at Salt Lake Cottages.

My partner Linda was born at Buckden. When I did my degree I was in the Dales at the time and travelling to Leeds every day. I don't particularly like cities and it had always been in the back of my mind to be able to work in the Dales. I didn't really want to leave the countryside and this arrangement is ideal. I don't go through one traffic light when I drive here to work!

Philip: If you're feeling a bit undisciplined here and you're getting sick of sitting at your desk with the same sort of view – nice as it is – you can go home and enjoy the novelty of working from home... We go and visit clients in cities and in terms of premises I always find them very depressing except for the very slick corporate ones and even they are a bit sterile and can give you a headache. But I don't feel at all depressed here on a Sunday night when I'm going to work on a Monday.

Simon: We can access the Internet from a mobile phone. I have two phone lines at home. We can re-direct the office phones, pile a load of files on to the laptop and go home if necessary so I can work quite happily at home too and so we do have that flexibility. Even in winter we can go outside the office if we want a break and you can feel some air and hear the robins sing and watch the squirrels. We've had pairs of deer walking through the car park. You're just not going to get that in a city. I'm not saying we're all roses round the door. We see the countryside for what it is.

Philip: I could move back to a city if I had to. I know I could cope with it but it's not something I want to do.

Simon: One thing which may surprise you – up until very recently, we kept a paper based admin system and all our contacts, all our invoicing system, all our books were in good old traditional pen and ink. This little book here has all sorts of advantages – totally random access – portable – unlimited battery life – high resolution screen. What more could you want!

BLACKSMITHS David & Rachel Clements

David (35) and Rachel (29) Clements are blacksmiths in the market town of Settle. They have a son Oscar (2). David is carrying on a family tradition as his father is a blacksmith, like his own grandfather before him.

D avid: 'I trained as a designer at Hull College of Art, specialising in three dimensional design specifically for exhibition and museum. Metalwork was purely a hobby.

My great grandfather was an engineer/ blacksmith in the Midlands and my grandfather went into the motor trade. I've always been interested in repairing cars and motorcycles from an early age and had an interest in metalwork as a hobby.

I wanted to do sculpture but didn't get into the Fine Art course so I thought I'd do something more commercial. I worked in London for about four years in retail design and moved up the ranks to become one of five senior designers until I got disillusioned with London and the pace of life down there.

I travelled on a push bike across Europe with a friend and ended up in Australia where I spent eighteen months before coming back home to my parents at Kilnsey, Wharfedale in 1990 and wondering what to do next. I didn't want to go back down to London. It was then I saw an ad for employment training up at Malham Tarn, a year's course basically just building and labouring.

Rachel was a final year student up in Newcastle doing a degree in media production, specialising in script writing. She was trying to reduce her overdraft in the holidays working in the pub next door to my parents' home so we met either side of the bar.

The idea of the training at Malham was that you would get a job with the National Trust or go on an enterprise scheme which quite appealed to me. I'd learned quite a few new skills like dry stone walling and I was really keen to do as many courses as I could with them because they paid your tuition. I was living with my parents so it was a really good opportunity to learn new skills.

One project was particularly good for me – they had a workshop with some welding equipment and a load of broken fence. I happened to mention over a cup of tea that I could weld so I ended up repairing the fencing. I had acquired some of my great grandfather's tools which we'd kept for sentimental reasons – we never throw anything away! I decided to dig out some of those old scroll tools out, knock up some garden gates and combine the dry stone walling with a bit of landscaping and building and start up a new business called Boundary Designs.

I had a LandRover and a trailer and all the gear, complete with the checked shirt and thought this is the life! I'd just started when a friend was buying the old smithy at Austwick. It was a petrol station combined with a car workshop and what had originally been a blacksmith's with a forge. My friend thought I might be interested in going over to look at some tools which had been left.

I couldn't believe the gear! There were shelves full of things and my eyes were just popping out of my head. I asked what he was doing with the workshop because the forge itself was a small room with an old stone forge and a huge pile of scrap in the middle built up over the years. My eyes lit up at the things lying against the walls. His intention was to convert the back which had been used for car repairs into a joinery shop. He suffered from ME at the time so everything was on hold. He said how about leasing the forge from me with idea that I'd make the gates there. I thought, why not have a go at forging? I'd enquired about going on a week long course run by the Rural Development Commission and because I was on the Enterprise scheme, it was subsidised.

David and Rachel Clements at work in the Settle forge

I went on the course at Harrogate and it was really enlightening. The tutor was fantastic, John Hill who had a forge in East Yorkshire. He was into restoring cars as well so we both had similar interests. I still had a book which I'd been given by a close friend when I was about seventeen which is almost a bible to blacksmiths called *The Edge of the Anvil* by an American author called Jack Andrews. It features a blacksmith called Samuel Yellin who revived forge work in the States about the turn of the century.

That book inspired me. He treated the iron as though it was Plasticine.

I was really fired up and anxious to get going into forging. I'd cleared the workshop out and you don't need very much to start up, just the forge fired from coke. Air is blasted through the coke to give the intense heat and the steel bar is pushed into the fire. Very rapidly it reaches a nice yellow heat and you can then manipulate it, draw it out, stretch it, bend it, squash it back together. Hand bellows are now replaced by an electric fan which blows air, with a big tap handle to control it. All you need is that, hammers of varying weights, depending on how fit you are and what you want to achieve, and an anvil to place your hot bar on. Everything is done with the hammer, the heat and the anvil. The less technology you have, quite often the better the forging. We would rather forge using the traditional skills we've learned. It's very labour intensive.

Rachel: By this time I had finished my course in Newcastle and moved back to Yorkshire. My mother was living in Kettlewell and I didn't know what I wanted to do. I could still script write without necessarily being employed by somebody but also I realised I didn't want to be stuck in a room all day by myself writing. David was working extremely hard to set his business up and was taking a lot of time and I asked if I could help at weekends. I was working in another pub by then and we had a house together at Coniston Cold so it was halfway between home and Austwick.

I offered my services – painting things, tidying up and bashing things – really nice jobs! I started doing this on a regular basis and I really quite enjoyed it. I loved the idea of working with David on our own and we found we worked very well together straight away. I thought well, why can't I do it? I'd had a go at forging and hammering things. Once we had cleared the workshop out and lit the forge then naturally in a small village word spread and the library bus would be parked outside. People were continually coming in wishing us good luck and asking us to do jobs. David was getting lots of little repair jobs and without really trying, he was getting too busy and needed some help.

I then decided I would come and work full time – I hated my pub job! Things were quite tight money wise because although we had all this work we weren't charging very much – which David still has a problem with! We started getting busier and I really loved it. I tried to get on a course similar to the one David had done although by then all the courses were being run down in Salisbury. To meet the criteria for the course you had to be working full time for a year as an assistant to a blacksmith just to show your commitment and that you'd picked up some basic techniques because they didn't want absolute novices.

While we were at Austwick we were told this premises was for sale in Settle and the house with it. We dreamed of buying it but there was absolutely no way we could afford it. Buying this was just a pipe dream but a while afterwards we were approached by the selling agent who had somebody interested in buying the property who wanted it to remain a blacksmith's shop but they needed somebody to run it. They asked if we would be willing to rent it, which was a fantastic opportunity for us. Not only that, the workshop is almost twice the size.

Richard: We don't do farrier work which involves a long apprenticeship, four or five years. Traditionally if you were a blacksmith, you were a blacksmith and farrier and you did both. If you're just a farrier your working career is only about eighteen years because it's so physically demanding.

People often ask if our work is dangerous. They see you handling a red hot bar of steel and think you must get burned all the time but you very quickly learn once you've picked up the hot bar not to do it again! A red hot bar isn't too bad because that will burn and if you let go, it cauterises the skin but if you pick up a black hot bar which is still hot enough to burn it will stick to your hand. We do get nasty little burns because as you're hitting the bars it has scale on it which can splash on to you. If the bar is very hot, you should use tongs. On the hearth we probably have about fifty different tongs, all for different sizes and sections of steel.

Rachel worked in the forge until two days before their son Oscar was born - and was back at work a month later

David and Rachel with a table, shield and candlestick made by Rachel. The table won awards at the Great Yorkshire Show

worn away to almost nothing but you put your feet on that piece of wood and believe it or not, it insulates. I've had some clogs made which helped but I couldn't get used to walking in them. We have a steep wooden staircase and I was tripping over all the time. Also, they don't have steel toecaps which you really need.

Alf Limmer, our predecessor, retired after fifty years in this workshop. He started when he was fourteen as an apprentice and he still comes to see us which is wonderful. I came into the workshop to see him when it was up for sale and I was very nervous but he was so encouraging, very forthcoming with information and certain techniques. When we came here we retained a lot of his old contacts so we were coming into an existing business with his goodwill as well.

Rachel's a really good blacksmith, she's really good at forging. I do the designing and when someone comes in with an idea I have a pretty good idea of what they want.

Considering that from the time we opened the door we've never had to look for work so there's obviously a need for us. We're busy and always have been.

Rachel: 'Our son Oscar was two in March (1999). I worked up untill the Friday and had him on the Sunday. It didn't stop me forging at all. My father-in-law is a blacksmith over at Kilnsey and he had a big commission for some very decorative gates at Coniston Cold church which are all traditionally made. I was perhaps slower running up and down the stairs and bending got a bit difficult in the end but otherwise I was fine. I had exactly a month off and then started going back when Oscar was asleep. We have an intercom and grandparents are very, very useful! I work three days a week now which is brilliant.

The locals have all been very supportive and we're both doing a job we very much enjoy. I don't know whether Oscar will follow in our footsteps but we hope there will be a blacksmith's here for many, many years to come.

The beauty of our job is that we can actually make tools to do specific jobs. A lot of the tools look rough and ready but they're purely for our use, they're not for sale. They're made very quickly and if they break we repair them or make another one. So the workshop is cluttered with tools we use for one specific job.

We wear ear defenders if we're using angle grinders and the power hammer can be noisy. It's one of the hazards of the job. You talk to old blacksmiths and they're often fairly deaf. We wear goggles as well to protect our eyes.

The worst aspect is cold. The floor is stone and the forge fire is at table height so even in winter you're sweating wearing just a T-shirt but your feet are freezing. The workshop is about a hundred years old. The anvil is set into stone flags and although I've replaced it, it's in the same position, standing on a stump of oak which is buried into the ground to make it solid. Next to that is a 1ft by 3ft bulk of wood, three inches thick which has

SCHOOL CHAPLAIN Norman Daniels

Norman Daniels (60), former chaplain of Giggleswick School, is now the vicar in charge of All Saints Parish, Keighley where he lives with his wife Elizabeth. Their son Andrew is a supermarket manager at Menston and daughter Susan is married with two children and teaches English at a sixth form college.

I'm not a Yorkshireman. I was born and bred in Belfast and the family came over to Settle when I was nine in 1947. I won a scholarship as a day boy to Giggleswick School. I went to Catteral Hall the junior school in 1949, then senior school from '51 to '57 and on to Leeds University to read history.

On my graduation I taught in Leeds for five years then in Singapore with the army school for six years, then I offered myself for ordination and came back to England in 1971 and went to St Michaels College Llandaff where I was ordained in 1973. I was in a parish in South Wales until '76 then I got a post as chaplain of a British army school at Rheindahlen, West Germany where I spent six years before returning to the Dales.

My parents, who lived in Settle, were getting no younger so I was looking for a parish as close as I could get when I saw the advert for a chaplain at Giggleswick School. I held the post from 1982 to '92, then I came down here to All Saints parish at Keighley and I've been here ever since.

A parish priest is quite a different job from that of a school chaplain. During term time I used to call it salvation by perspiration, you never really stopped. I taught games, hockey to the senior girls' team in the winter and spring and golf for the rest of the spring and summer terms. At one time I was careers advisor, as well as teaching general studies and history, running the sixth form club – we had a bar Saturday night and Sunday lunchtime – and the Christian Union and all the things a chaplain does.

The chaplain's cottage was very well placed near the school buildings. A chaplain has a very important role in a boarding school because when children want to unburden themselves about something and they don't want their parents, their headmaster or housemaster or their peers to know, they know the chaplain is the only person who cannot tell. They knew they could approach the cottage at any time of the day or night. Any school chaplain worth his salt should have enough secrets in his head to blow the school apart but unfortunately you can't tell any of them!

I'll give you an example of a typical day – at Giggleswick we had games Tuesdays, Thursdays and Saturdays in the afternoons so you only taught for half of these days. I never got used to teaching Saturday mornings, it didn't seem right. Mondays, Wednesdays and Fridays were full days so my typical Wednesday started with breakfast duty at quarter past seven then lessons all Wednesday morning then I'd have a confirmation class for Catteral Hall at 2 o'clock and another for senior school at quarter past three then I'd be teaching from 4 o'clock until six. I had a Christian Union group before prayers which started at half past seven, house prayers at nine followed by an indoor hockey practice in the sports hall until half past ten or so. When I had a pint in the Black Horse at twenty to eleven, I thought I'd earned it.

The days were like that but the beauty about the job was that it was very varied. The only trouble was, the pupils stay the same age, they get to eighteen and leave but you keep getting older and it becomes harder and harder!

When I first arrived at Giggleswick the first head I worked for said everybody had to attend chapel whatever their denomination but he didn't want anyone who wasn't confirmed in chapel so we used to have a special service at the same time in the assembly hall for the Great Unwashed. I decided it wasn't fair that I should take the Eucharist all the time in chapel so

Norman Daniels (Back Row, left) enjoyed teaching golf during his stint at Giggleswick. This was just one of the many groups to benefit from his expertise

once a term I decided I'd do the one in the assembly hall and get a local priest to do the one in chapel. The assembly hall at Giggleswick in those days had deep purple woodwork, scarlet curtains, pink walls and it really was frightening. The first time I took the service, I came out afterwards with the headmaster who said it had been very nice and I said, 'Well, I didn't think so, that hall is a terrible place to worship. Whoever thought of that colour scheme wants shooting.' He said, 'I chose it.'

We established good relations with the parish which was nice and once a term they came to evensong in the school chapel and once a term the confirmed went down to the parish church for the evening service. My wife Elizabeth was also first lady warden at Giggleswick Parish Church and had duties at the girls' houses as well so she was always involved.

Giggleswick is a good school and a nice place to teach. From the point of view of discipline it was the easiest ride I ever had in my teaching career. There was no comparison with teaching in an inner city school in a rough area. For instance, on a

Norman Daniels at Giggleswick where leading worship was only one of his many duties

Saturday morning we used to have congregational practice just after breakfast in the chapel to go through the hymns we would be singing on Sunday and the rest of the week. The first time I went, there were about 285 kids there. They weren't familiar with the hymn so they were told to hum the tune and I couldn't believe it when they all did... in an inner city there would have been ructions. Giggleswick is also a very good school musically and we used to sing with the United choirs at Ripon Cathedral and sang evensong at Liverpool Cathedral.

Catteral Hall, the junior school at Giggleswick, like most country houses had a great sweeping staircase leading down to the front door which was strictly out of bounds to children, only staff could use it. Russell Harty, who also taught at Giggleswick, told me the story about a little boy who had run away one night. They'd found him and brought him back at two in the morning and Russell was asking him how he'd managed to sneak out. He explained, 'I put my pyjamas on over my day clothes and matron didn't notice. When everybody was asleep I got out of bed and took my pyjamas off and I got through a window into the sewing room, then I went down through a trap door into the games room, went along the corridor, found my way down into the cellar and opened the trap door from the coal hole and climbed out of the window.' Russell asked him why he hadn't just gone down the stairs and out of the front door. 'I couldn't do that,' the little boy said, 'it's against the rules.'

All teachers are old and if you're over 35 you're not only past it you've never been there in the first place. If you have a collar and grey hair then you become a sort of sexless angel. It's quite amazing. We had two scholars every year from the English Speaking Youth Fellowship. One American girl decided she would try field hockey and the first session was in the sports hall. She was following the captain of hockey and they didn't know the head of games was right behind them. This American girl saw me in a track suit with a hockey stick and said, 'Gee, are we being taught by a man?' and our captain said without blinking, 'That's not a man, that's the chaplain.'

There was another time we were doing hockey practice in the hall and this very attractive young girl started getting changed while I was talking to them. When I told her off she said it was OK as there were no boys around. I said, 'No, but I'm here' and she said she didn't think I mattered...

Over the ten years, I knew every child by his or her Christian name and apart from the overseas parents, I knew all the parents as well. Giggleswick School is a nice family caring atmosphere. After I left, my mother was in a nursing home up there and we used to take her for days out. We were going through Giggleswick one day and she asked me 'Do you miss school?' It was one of those days when the sleet was lancing nearly horizontal, it was freezing cold and we were just passing the sports field where the girls were playing hockey and I thought, yes, but there's some days I miss it more than others!

I enjoyed hockey but teaching golf was a little more pleasant in that the sun was generally on your back. I played hockey at University and the army turned me into a coach. I got an elementary teaching certificate for golf. My handicap was eleven when I was at Giggleswick. I can't get out so much now and it's up to nineteen. One of the things I set up at Giggleswick – and they still do it – was to run the scoreboard at the Open. It's a marvellous week, I miss that.

When I was a boy there was a tradition that every pupil attempted the Three Peaks before he left. We walked it for charity and the last time I did it it took me eight and three quarter hours which wasn't bad. The main thing I remember from the Dales when we were kids is some of the rambles and some of the sport. We toured in Spain with the hockey but the first hockey tour we took was to Amsterdam and Hamburg. There was myself, Mrs Fox the housemaster's wife and eighteen girls. Our hotel in Amsterdam was right in the middle of the red light district.

All our matches were at 5 or 6 o'clock in the evenings so our days, apart from the training sessions, were free. This particular morning we'd been on a canal trip and when we got back, most of the girls wanted to go shopping except four who said they would rather go to Anne Frank House so I said I'd take them. This was half past eleven in the morning and we were walking through Amsterdam. We passed what I thought was a milliners because they had semi-dressed and naked statues in the window then as we passed one of the girls said, 'That statue moved!' I shepherded them past quickly but one of the girls had a wicked sense of humour. When we met the others for lunch back at the hotel she said, 'Mrs Fox, we went past a brothel and all the women were beckoning so the chaplain went back to have another look!

Because we were a small school we had the 'major minor' sport rule that all boys had to play rugby if required in the winter term and all girls had to play hockey. If they were excused hockey or rugby then they could choose one of the minor sports like squash, netball, golf or tennis. In the summer term all boys had to play cricket if required and the girls tennis so I didn't get some of my best golfers because they were required for cricket and tennis. Pupils who weren't sporting could elect to do a stint on community service because there was built in community service programme which I was involved with as well.

In a parish, apart from school assemblies and funerals, you can organise your time better whereas at school you're governed by bells. In a parish like All Saints, your boss is the Bishop of Bradford and Bradford's a long way away but in a school, you look round and the headmaster's right behind you! It was a cultural shock moving from the Dales to Keighley. There's a joke told which is very close to the truth – a guy had a puncture just opposite the church. He had the car jacked up and was just taking the wheel off when two fellas started opening his bonnet. He asked them what they were doing and they said, 'Well, if you're having the wheels, we'll have the engine.'

I'm terrible for losing my car keys but at Giggleswick I never lost them because I left them in the ignition no matter where I was going, even shopping to Settle. All Saints Parish is very much like a Little England in microcosm. We've got inner city deprivation, a large ethnic minority, part of the rough working class estates as well as middle class and upper class areas.

Sermons were a bit more difficult in Giggleswick than in the parish because the first Sunday in the month was the whole school from the 7-year olds to the 19-year olds plus the staff. I didn't attempt to speak to anybody but the young ones and used to tell them stories. The older children enjoyed it better than their own service. The second Sunday was evening service and that was just the senior school. You've got to be punchy – I rarely exceeded eight minutes. You've got to get your point over quickly.

We have a big ministry team here at All Saints. There are two readers and a curate plus two parish worship assistants, the director of diocesan education and myself and the lady canon of the cathedral so ten minutes is the absolute maximum they're not allowed to stray beyond. If they talk for longer than that, they won't be asked again. If you can't say what you've got to say in ten minutes you've either got a lot to say or you're taking too long to say it.

I've resisted technology and computers – I use a word-processor but they're going to buy us all a fax modem whatever that is and I'm dreading it. At least when mail drops through the door I pick it up, bin what I don't want and file what I do but I'll never find it in that thing and that worries me. I'm hoping if I retire at 65 I'll get away with it.

We still have a house in Settle and so we might retire there. It's a lovely place to live.

QUARRY MANAGER Bob Orange

Bob Orange (41) is Operations Manager at Pioneer's Coldstones Quarry, close to the village of Greenhow, 3 miles from Pateley Bridge. Bob lives at Boroughbridge and has an 11-year old daughter Madeleine and an 8-year old son Nicholas.

Greenhow has been a mining and quarrying area for centuries, going back to pre-Roman times when the main mineral extracted was lead. By the end of the 19th century, the miners had turned from mining lead to mining fluorspar, a mineral that was used for the glass and steel industries and is still extracted on our site for use in the modern chemical industry.

There is evidence that limestone quarrying has taken place on Coldstones Hill for at least two centuries. The original quarries produced lime for agriculture and an 18th century plan shows several lime kilns in the area. The building of the railway to Pateley Bridge stimulated the lime business and several large kilns were set up. The largest of these, built in the 1860s can still be seen at Toft Gate in the fields to the east of us. Lime would be taken from here by cart to the rail terminus at Pateley Bridge, Coldstones limestone was being used for roadstone in the early 19th century as well as for agricultural and mortar lime. In 1820 it was used in the construction of the Pateley Bridge to Skipton road. In the early days rock would be transported to the roadside and then broken. By 1900 rock was being broken up on site using hammers and quarry workers were paid by the tonnage broken. It wasn't until 1929 that money was invested in stone crushing machinery and gelignite was used for breaking the rock. During the war large tonnages were used for making aerodrome runways in and around the North Yorkshire area. In 1985 Pioneer decided to invest over £1million in new plant and today we produce just short of a million tonnes of aggregate a year.

I've been at the quarry eighteen years and my official title is Operations Manager. The quarry is open from 6am until about 5.30pm, five and a half days a week. Every day is different and that's what makes the job fun. My job involves dealing with people, both within the quarry and in the local community, health and safety and generally running the business. I have an assistant manager, a foreman and other staff to do all the hard work, I just keep the whole thing ticking over, keep the plates spinning on the poles as it were. We have 24 direct employees and we employ a lot of sub-contractors and about fifty hauliers. It's a busy quarry, probably joint second largest in North Yorkshire.

Dealing with people is not always an easy job. You have to be tactful trying to tell a guy who's being doing something for twenty years that there is a better way of doing it in such a way as not to upset him. In today's world you don't demand that people do things, it's talked about, you ask the right questions and usually they know the correct procedures.

Safety is always an important factor. Nowadays, it's about deciding the jobs that need doing, assessing how dangerous these jobs will be and what needs to be done to minimise the dangers. In the past more emphasis was placed on protecting the person with guards and so on. This is still important of course, guards, protective gear, high visibility coats and hard hats are all used, but the correct attitude to safety and the assessment of risk to minimise danger is the way forward. There are very few quarrying accidents these days compared to the days when hand hammers were used and blasting techniques were more primitive, but because of the size of machinery if there were to be an accident it would probably be serious.

Bob Orange is Operations Manager at Coldstones Quarry, probably the highest quarry in England

We're probably the highest quarry in England – the height above sea level is 410m at the top of the quarry bund and 345m in the quarry bottom. We have some very interesting weather! The winters haven't been so bad recently but going back years there used to be about a fortnight at a time when transport couldn't get in. They could get to Pateley Bridge and Greenhow but the last few hundred yards would be white out. One of the experienced shotfirers remembers a year when there was a snow blow and a total white out. The only way for him to find his way back to the office was to walk along the stockpiles checking the sizes of the stone. He knew where the 20mm pile was and he knew where the 40mm pile was so he used these to check the direction he was walking in, otherwise he would have just had to stand there. It needn't even be snowing for us to have a white out here, sometimes the wind is so strong there can be a white out just with snow blowing off the ground.

We have a lot of problems with the wind. This is one of the few sites I know that has to put wind sheets up to protect the drivers while they are trying to sheet their loads. (All wagons are sheeted to keep the dust down.) The wind can be so strong that it can blow men off the top of the wagons and that could be quite nasty – it's a long way down!

When we bought the last drill rig, the operator had a choice of having an all-singing, all dancing cabin for the rig or the open air rig. He chose to have an open air rig, he didn't want to get soft sitting in a cabin. He's spent all his life on Greenhow and he wouldn't have it any other way.

This quarry will keep going for about another 25 years. Quarrying is always an issue with environmentalists. A big part of my job is environmentally related and we do try to keep things right, trying to keep the dust within the quarry and so on. The site has been screened all the way round by constructing and seeding an artificial bank or bund. This helps retain the shape of the hill as well as hiding the quarry. This is a beautiful area and the aim is not to spoil it. You could drive past this place and hardly realise it was here if it weren't for the signs. There are SSSI's (Sites of Special Scientific Interest) all around us and when we were planning to extend this site in 1992 this was one of the things which held us up. Where the old miners had tipped all their waste the soil was contaminated with lead and only certain plants can grow on the poisoned ground of their spoil tips. By definition these are quite rare plants which only grow in the old mining areas. A condition of the planning permission was that these plants were relocated. Seeds were taken and they were re-grown in greenhouses and brought back to the quarry to be replanted on the new quarry bund. We even get botanists to come up every now and then to monitor their growth.

Going back twenty years quarries were all over the place and they just used to tip their rubbish outside. This is quite rightly no longer acceptable – quarries should be good neighbours to everybody. The only quarrying messes around now should be historical messes! Generally, the industry is getting its act together. We had an Open Day in June when we had about

600 people round and we didn't have one single complaint. We sent out invitations to everybody at this end of the Dale and gave guided tours with members of staff to explain what we do and how we do it. The public were able to see all the machinery close at hand. Everybody was surprised by the size of the quarry which lies hidden within the hill. They couldn't believe that something this large could be so well hidden.. It has even been suggested that we bring tourists in to do tours on a regular basis.

All the transport from the quarry used to go out from here straight through the village until we put in the new road to by-pass Greenhow village. This has been a great improvement for the residents. We do get occasional complaints from the villagers about blasting, this is understandable, but although they feel the vibrations the measurements are very, very low – below 1 PPV (our limit is 8 PPV) and vibrations only start to damage property at about 50 PPV. The vibration levels we produce are far too low to damage the houses but feeling any movement upsets people. We monitor every blast so if any one is unhappy about a particular blast they can ring us and get the measurements. We talk to the locals and they accept our explanations but they will never like feeling the blasts.

Some people do hate quarrying, not in my back yard and that sort of attitude, but they don't realise that quarrying supports a large part of their lives. It's fundamental! There is virtually nothing anybody does that doesn't involve quarrying in one way or another. If they are walking in a town they will be walking on quarried products, if they are at home or work most people will live in buildings constructed from quarried materials and many will also use quarried products in various ways in their everyday lives. There are only two ways of getting raw materials to make or produce anything and that is either growing it or digging it out of the ground. People who think we don't need mines and quarries forget that their cars are probably made of 90 percent mined or quarried material and their houses even more.

If you take away the things from houses that have been mined or quarried you are left with timber window frames and the plastic coating on your wires. You would have to take away your roof tiles, the glass from your windows – many people don't realise that glass is made from silica sand and limestone, the plaster and plasterboard covering your walls, the paint from your window frames, the bricks, concrete or stone which make up the walls and the roads and paths to your property. There are also many hidden uses of quarried materials for example most make-up has limestone filler as does toothpaste, sugar is also manufactured using limestone.

People also forget that you can only quarry limestone where the limestone is found. We do a school education programme where we go round visiting schools for half a day. Then they visit the quarry for a full day. We let them stand in the bucket of the loading shovel (switched-off of course) and watch the rocks going through the primary crusher. The aim of our schools work is so the local children understand why quarries are where they are and what happens inside our quarry. Shirley who now does the school work with me had shown me some letters that children living near another quarry had written 'We don't like quarries', 'We think quarries should be put in towns', 'We think quarries ought to be in waste tips, because they are already messy'. They'd seen a TV documentary which had done an inaccurate job in explaining the fundamental principles behind quarrying. It made me angry to think that they'd done all this derogatory stuff about quarrying. We try to explain to our local children that we are here because this is where the rock is, that people in the modern world are using limestone to make concrete, hardcore, car parks, and roads. We are not involved in any major road building programs and sell to many different customers who are constructing things like new housing estates, supermarkets, hospital car parks and so on.

Many of the limestone areas of the world are beautiful, Yorkshire is no exception, but limestone is also one of the main rocks that is needed for construction. There are increasingly more problems obtaining permission to quarry in scenic areas but this is often the only place where they can quarry for hard rock. This area will have a problem in 25 years time when our permission runs out because the other large local quarries also run out of stone. So that's 4 million tonnes a year just going to go, and as there are no more permissions allowed in the National Park how will our children meet their needs? It makes you wonder where the rock's going to come from. The Scandinavians would love to ship it across but I wouldn't have thought that would help our economy. I will be retired then but it'll be watching to see what happens...

Coldstones Quarry is owned by Pioneer Aggregates (UK) Ltd

FISHERIES OFFICER Neil Handy

NEIL HANDY (35) is a Fisheries Enforcement Officer working for the Environment Agency. He lives in North Ribblesdale with wife Sarah and son Joseph who was born in July 1998. His working area covers the north west central belt from North Liverpool up to Shap as well as through the Fylde, Lancaster and Southport and the job includes licence checking, fish rescue and anti-poaching.

I've always had a love of water and fish. My dad tells me that when I was eighteen months old I was stood at the side of him by the river when he was talking to a farming rep. Next thing I'd gone and as he turned around I was just disappearing under the water. He dragged me out and ever since he couldn't keep me away from water although you would have thought that experience would have had the opposite effect!

I can remember my gran taking me out on reins down the beck side holding me just far enough away so I could put a worm through to catch fish. An old chap from the village used to take me ferreting. To me it was a normal country life – hunting, shooting and fishing. I caught my first salmon when I was ten years old.

As kids, when we were about twelve, we used to set off at about 9 o'clock at night with a rod apiece and a bucket of worms and go eel fishing. At 2 or 3 o'clock in the morning there'd be torches shining and it'd be my dad looking for me. We used to try and sneak home and climb in the back window and pretend we'd been in bed but we didn't always get away with it!

My interest in this job goes back to when I was about 15. I used to fish down at Stainforth Foss and Len Idiens who was the North West Water river bailiff at the time got me interested in coming out and working with them at nights. I started going with them when they were catching brood stock for the hatchery. Every year they would strip eggs off the salmon and put them into the hatchery for rearing to put back into rivers.

In 1984 I started working for them as a reserve or call-out bailiff looking for salmon poachers. You get your adrenaline running a bit but it was like second nature. It was mainly night work or early morning but I was getting paid for something I really enjoyed doing. Unfortunately in 1994 Len's health failed and I was asked if I wanted to do a three month job from September to the end of December bailiffing at the top of the river in spawning time. There were no assurances or guarantees that there would be any work after that.

For three years I worked on short contracts but I got involved with all the other aspects of bailiffing such as fish rescues where there was pollution and fish were in distress, licence checking, removing fish from total drain down – if they were draining a pond out for building, we would move the fish elsewhere. There were a lot of different aspects but they all intermingle.

As far as pollution is concerned, the Ribble is reasonably good. There's always going to be incidences of pollution wherever you've got any type of industry but it's relatively a very clean river. We have salmon and grayling and crayfish which need clean water.

Our work has recently been split into two sections. There's an enforcement side which is what I do and the other side is science, who do things like habitat restoration, tree planting, fencing areas of river and doing surveys to monitor areas which are recovering from pollution or to see how things are doing in general in case as a safeguard for the future.

We can be called out at any time in a working day from 1 o'clock in the morning until midnight and we do a lot of travelling but I enjoy it all. I enjoy the night work and early mornings which to me are the best times of the day because there's nobody else about.

You see an awful lot at night you wouldn't see in daytime –

badgers, foxes, deer, mink, rats, voles, herons fishing in the dark... That's one of the beauties of the job – when you're out on the river you're not just looking at fish, it's everything that's around you. Kingfishers have done really well this year. It's very rare for me to go out without seeing one.

I've had a 4ft otter swim up to me at night when I was fly fishing. It came up right next to me and I was up to my chest in a pair of waders. I could have literally patted it on the head. The old keepers tell you stories about years gone by when they would trap an otter a week. There were always plenty around then they vanished for various different reasons but they've made a comeback to certain rivers now. But the number of otters that we have in our area, they're welcome to a few fish, they're not like poachers!

If you catch poachers at night they usually come reasonably quietly. You might have to chase them to catch them but I've never come across any violence although I know it has happened in certain areas. We tend to get more hassle checking rod licences but then again we're checking so many that the confrontation levels give you more chance of running into somebody that's going to be awkward.

You get people trying to fish without permission, some coming with nets and trying to take fish when the water's really low in the middle of daytime. My job is to take evidence and inform them that they're committing an offence. We will caution them and in severe cases we can arrest them. The facts are then reported to my area office and from then on it's decided whether or not they go to court. In most instances they do then it's entirely in the hands of the magistrates or judge depending on how serious it is whether it's the Crown Court or the Magistrates Court. There's no set amount for fines.

Anti-poaching involves a lot of sneaking about but there are places where you stand a good chance of finding them...

Neil Hardy at Stainforth Foss where he started fishing as a schoolboy

At nights during the hours of darkness there has to be two of you for obvious reasons, insurance and health and safety. There are seven of us full time enforcement officers and I can be working with any one of them and any one of a number of lads that do what I started doing, coming out on anti-poaching. They're nearly all fishermen and have an interest in looking after the future.

You have to keep quiet and there's no smoking – you can't give yourselves away either by sight, smell or sound. I suppose being out in the dark would be frightening to anyone who wasn't used to it but with growing up in the country and spending so much time out fishing or shooting it's a part of my life.

One night an inspector was standing at a fence when an owl actually landed on his head. By all accounts, he didn't even move! Another of my mates had been looking through the equipment we have for seeing in the dark and had seen a Sika stag approaching. When it got to within about two yards he gave the night sight to his colleague and said just have a look round and see what you can see. He pulled it away from his eye to clean the lens and the Sika stag screamed and nearly frightened him to death.

I've had scary moments, not just as a bailiff but as an angler. I was actually thirteen before I learned to swim and that was in Stainforth Foss. The Foss is a very popular place but I've seen numerous people pulled out of there that have been virtually drowned. There have been at least half a dozen pulled out by anglers while I've been there. We used to warn people not to go in in certain conditions but they used to think we didn't want them there just because we were fishing.

This wet summer's been bad for anybody wanting to swim but it's been a good year for me for the fish. We've had so many dry summers that they've taken away 50 percent of the area that you could rear fish in. No fly or aquatic life will survive unless it's under water so you're taking away 50percent of the food. So many things have an effect on fish population.

In the late seventies and early eighties mink were quite a bad problem on the river. When I first became a bailiff we trapped 89 in six months for the Ministry. Over the years they've been thinned out but there are other predators like goosanders which have increased tenfold in the past ten years, certainly in the upper reaches. I've seen creches of up to thirty. Get one of them sweeping though one of these little pools and they can soon wipe a lot of fish out. We even get cormorants up as far up as Newhouses Tarn and Cam Beck which are more thought of as a bird which sticks around estuaries. And there are a lot of herons.

Salmon runs have gone down seriously certainly since the late eighties probably by 75 percent but this year's looking a bit more promising. It's probably down to the fact that there's been a lot of water so the small fish have more protection especially on the river because it's so peaty and cormorants, goosanders and herons can't take them to the same extent.

Sometimes you see things you wouldn't believe if you hadn't seen them for yourself. I once watched a bloke casting upstream. There was only one tree on the bank and he hit it three times in three casts. I was on the other side of the river thinking 'You've no chance'. The next cast went into the water and he got a seven pound salmon and lo and behold with the next cast he got another one so from looking like he hadn't a

hope in hell he ended up with two salmon on the bank.

A Scottish lad came fishing one year and he put a piece of orange peel on his hook and hooked a salmon. He lost it but then he hooked another one. I can only assume it was the colour. At the end of September the salmon start to get more aggressive towards reds which is the colour of the other cock fish.

The best fish I've caught was one this year, just short of eleven pounds but the biggest I've caught was nineteen and a half, a salmon about ten years ago. I've caught barble on the River Ure which I've never caught before. I was actually fishing for grayling. The barble's sometimes known as the fresh water salmon, they're a coarse fish and fight very strongly and it's good sport fishing but I prefer to catch salmon and sea trout.

I've caught my ears several times fly fishing. I read the other day about somebody catching a swift when fishing at night. My eldest brother caught bats a couple of times when he was fly fishing. I've heard of somebody catching a cow at night sea trout fishing. It set off up the field and the hook snapped off. The following day he had to go up to the farm when the cows came in for milking and look for his fly before the farmer found it.

In the bad weather in winter there's still all the redd counting to do when the salmon spawn. We go out and count how many pairs have been there. We can do that on freezing days as long as we can see.

A lot of the job is just knowing that stretch of water. Every river's different. When we go away for a few days it's always near a river. I always have to stop and see if there's anything worth looking at.

I owe a lot to my mentor Len who was who sadly passed away recently. He taught me all I know. Every day you go out you learn something. One of the great things is you meet a lot of people. 95 percent of them are a good crack and you have a common denominator in fishing.

I'd love to see a lot more kids coming into it. They're the future not just for fishing but for the whole river environment because without people to look after it it's just going to deteriorate. It's still a great sport but it's just dying out.

I'm the eternal optimist – you have to be. When I started fishing for salmon at ten and eleven there were a lot more salmon about than there is now but I'm optimistic that these days will come back.